BETTER THAN BEEF

For my husband, Kevin,

who inspires me to believe that

nothing is impossible, and our family,

Aubrey, Taylor, Alex, Brianna, Ben, Max, and Theo,

My everything.

—K.B.

www.castlepointbooks.com

The Castle Point Books trademark is owned by Castle Point Publishing, LLC.
Castle Point books are published and distributed by St. Martin's Publishing Group.

ISBN 978-1-250-27376-5 (trade paperback)
ISBN 978-1-250-27377-2 (ebook)

Design by Joanna Williams
Photograph on page 2 and 138 used under license from Shutterstock.com.
All other photographs by Kristin Bryan.

Our books may be purchased in bulk for promotional, educational, or business use.
Please contact your local bookseller or the Macmillan Corporate and Premium Sales Department
at 1-800-221-7945, extension 5442, or by email at MacmillanSpecialMarkets@macmillan.com.

First Edition: 2021

10 9 8 7 6 5 4 3 2 1

BETTER THAN BEEF

THE PLANT-BASED MEAT COMFORT FOOD COOKBOOK

KRISTIN BRYAN

CASTLE POINT BOOKS
NEW YORK

CONT

ENTS

INTRODUCTION

There's not much that can make me happier than sitting around a table with the ones I love, enjoying a home-cooked meal like a big bowl of spaghetti and meatballs, Grandma's meatloaf, or a delicious burger. Whether you're a meat lover, vegetarian, or vegan, delicious food is a thing of joy.

I believe everyone should have this joy in life. For me, that means satisfying foods that are full of fresh, delicious ingredients that offer color, flavor, and comfort. These are the kinds of foods that bring family and friends together, building connections and launching new beginnings.

I began cooking plant-based meals at home when one of my daughters switched to a vegetarian diet. Food is at the core of who I am, so it's essential for me to learn and evolve, not only as a culinarian, but also as the person responsible for feeding my family. With mostly meat lovers and one new vegetarian at the dinner table, I began to explore plant-based meals that everyone would enjoy. In my job as a chef, I had begun cooking with plant-based ground beef and noticed that it had become more available in local grocery stores. Plant-based meats changed everything for me as a chef and a mom. With access to these innovative and tasty new products, I began developing techniques and recipes that won over even my hard-core meat lovers.

I can empathize with home chefs everywhere when it comes to cooking with plant-based meats: It's a challenge to make veggies taste as delicious as a big, juicy hamburger. I spent a lot of time experimenting with ingredients, layering flavors, and finding methods that make it easy to work with plant-based meats. That's why I am so proud to share this collection: The recipes in *Better Than Beef* will offer you the ability to create delicious meals with plant-based and beef-substitute products without sacrificing any flavor. Inside you'll find a variety of breakfasts, lunches, appetizers, and dinners that are familiar, fresh, traditional and, most important, a little downhome.

With these dishes, you can bring your family and friends to the table, enjoy spending time together, and make memories one meal at a time. So here's to exploring new products and flavors, enjoying delicious comfort food, and savoring the moments we create in the process.

Kristin

A NOTE ABOUT INGREDIENTS

Salt

You'll notice I specify "flake" salt in some of the recipes. You can use regular salt instead, but flake salt (also called Maldon salt) has a less bitter flavor than regular salt. It's also a great finishing salt because it adds a dash of texture. Using it is a simple, non-fussy way to elevate food.

Pepper

Coarse black pepper will give your dishes a stronger pepper flavor and aroma. Finely ground pepper stays in the background, for a more subtle flavor. In a few recipes I specify coarse black pepper, but you can substitute with regular ground pepper.

Oils

I keep two kinds of oil in my pantry: organic cold pressed light olive oil and organic cold pressed extra virgin olive oil. Olive oil has a health benefit that makes it my personal choice. It also cooks well on high heat and I prefer the flavor. You can, however, substitute with your preferred oil.

Harissa

Harissa is a combination of spices, with the "star" of the seasoning show being dried ancho chili peppers. This spicy, aromatic blend originated in the Middle East and has become quite accessible. I can find both powder and paste forms at my local grocery store.

Chipotle

Regular chili powder is a blend of dried chilies, garlic, onion, and cumin. Chipotle powder is made from smoked jalapeño peppers that have been dried and crushed into a powder form. If you can't find chipotle powder, you can substitute with chili powder, but it will lack the smoky flavor.

Ground Beef Substitutes

Not all of the ground beef substitutes available on the market today will cook the same way, and not all of them will taste the same in these recipes. I would encourage you to experiment with different brands and settle on the taste and texture you prefer. (I almost always use a brand that most resembles regular ground beef. There are fewer smoky flavors present, so I'm able to layer and create custom flavors in each recipe.)

BREAKFAST

Egg and Chorizo Morning Scramble with Chive Crema

SERVES 4

The *Egg and Chorizo Morning Scramble* is a feisty little breakfast dish with flavor that will get your morning off to a fabulous start. There are several types of plant-based chorizo substitutes, and all of them are good options. For this recipe I used the plant-based chorizo in the casing, but you can use the crumbled chorizo. Chive crema adds a bright, crisp, and herbal flavor to complement the heat in the chorizo.

CHIVE CREMA

½ cup sour cream

1 teaspoon dried chives
(or ½–1 teaspoon chopped fresh chives)

SCRAMBLE

2 green onions

2 chorizo meat-substitute links
(or 1 10-ounce bag crumbled chorizo)

1 tablespoon olive oil

8 large eggs

2 tablespoons half-and-half or
heavy cream

2 tablespoons unsalted butter

TO MAKE THE CHIVE CREMA

1. Mix the sour cream and the chives in a small bowl to make the chive crema. Season with salt. Set aside.

TO MAKE THE SCRAMBLE

1. Chop the green onions. Set aside.

2. Remove the chorizo casings and break the chorizo into small pieces with your hands.

3. In a 9″ sauté pan, heat the olive oil and cook the chorizo over medium low heat, about 2–3 minutes. (If you're using crumbled chorizo, add ¼ cup of water while cooking.) Set aside.

4. Add eggs and half-and-half to a 7″ mixing bowl and gently beat the egg mixture with a fork until blended.

5. In a 9″ sauté pan, heat the butter over low heat. Add the egg mixture and use a wooden spoon to gently stir in the butter, creating a creamy egg base. As the egg begins to cook, slowly stir and fold in the green onions.

6. While the eggs are still moist, add the chorizo and continue cooking to your desired egg consistency.

7. Season with salt and pepper.

8. Divide the *Egg and Chorizo Morning Scramble* into 4 portions and top with the chive crema.

Note: This is a fun brunch dish. Serve family style with an extra side of chive crema and fresh mango or peach slices.

Breakfast Hash with Sweet Potatoes and Sweet Onion

SERVES 4

I adore brunch, so I'm always thinking of new, creative brunch dishes to serve friends and family. My breakfast hash is the perfect vegetarian brunch recipe. The sweet potatoes and onions become toasty and caramelized, and the beef substitute adds a depth of hearty flavor. I top each serving with an over-easy egg, which creates an irresistibly creamy sauce. The *Breakfast Hash with Sweet Potatoes and Sweet Onion* is a dish that will be in high demand with friends. I pair it with a fresh fruit and cheese board and bottomless peach mimosas. Now this is the way to end the week!

2 tablespoons olive oil

2 sweet potatoes, diced

1 large onion, diced

12 ounces ground beef substitute

½ teaspoon salt

½ teaspoon pepper

1 teaspoon onion powder

1½ cups spinach or watercress

½ tablespoon unsalted butter

4 large eggs

1 teaspoon chopped chives

1. In a 10″ skillet, heat the olive oil on medium heat.

2. Add the sweet potatoes and cook for 3–4 minutes. The sweet potatoes will still be firm.

3. Add the onion, ground beef substitute, salt, pepper, and onion powder to the sweet potatoes. Stir together and cook until the ground beef substitute has browned and the vegetables are tender. (If needed, you can add ¼ cup of water until the vegetables have cooked.)

4. When the mixture is finished, add the greens to the pan and lightly toss with the ground beef substitute mixture to coat the greens. Turn off the heat.

5. In a nonstick egg pan or 6″ skillet melt ½ tablespoon of butter on medium low heat. Add the sunny-side up eggs one at a time, and cook to your preference.

6. Divide the hash into 4 portions and top each with an egg.

7. Season with salt and pepper and garnish with the chives. Serve immediately.

Note: Save time by purchasing precut sweet potatoes and onions. To add more flavor, try toppings like sour cream, ranch dressing, or spicy mayonnaise.

Breakfast Taco Bar

SERVES 6

This breakfast taco bar is inspired by a little roadside taco bar in Napa that serves some of the most delectable breakfast tacos I've ever tasted. I decided to re-create it with my own personal touches and a ground chorizo substitute. This *Breakfast Taco Bar* makes my crew deliriously happy and gives me the satisfaction of knowing that I gave them a flavorful *and* healthy start to their day.

1 cup shredded cheddar cheese

1 cup pickled jalapeño peppers

1 cup diced tomatoes, (or use cherry tomatoes, halved)

1 large onion, diced

1 cup fresh spinach

1 avocado, sliced

1 package flour tortillas (10-12 in one package)

2 tablespoons olive oil

10 ounces ground chorizo substitute

2 tablespoons unsalted butter

8 large eggs

¼ cup half-and-half or whole milk

½ teaspoon salt

½ teaspoon pepper

½ cup sour cream (optional)

1. Preheat the oven to 250 degrees F.

2. Prepare your taco bar by setting out cheese, jalapeño, tomatoes, onion, spinach, and avocado in small serving bowls.

3. Wrap the tortillas in aluminum foil, and place them in the oven while preparing the remaining taco bar ingredients.

4. In an 8″ skillet, heat the olive oil. Add the ground chorizo substitute, and cook until warmed through. Place in a serving bowl and cover.

5. In a separate 8″ skillet, melt the butter on medium to low heat.

6. In a medium mixing bowl, beat the eggs with the half-and-half or milk, and pour the mixture into the warmed skillet.

7. Add salt and pepper to the eggs, stirring vigorously to create a creamy scramble. When cooked to desired consistency, turn into a serving bowl and cover.

8. Place all of the taco bar ingredients on your table or kitchen island. Take the warmed tortillas out of the oven, and your breakfast taco bar is open! Serve immediately.

Note: I often serve with a side of sour cream. Other good additions are Sriracha sauce and chipotle mayonnaise.

Sausage Frittata with Caramelized Onions

SERVES 4–6

The frittata, an Italian version of an omelet, is a fabulous way to create a quick breakfast, lunch, or dinner. I can't remember when I started making frittata, but it has become my go-to meal when I need to use up extra sauces, vegetables, meats, or cheeses. I created this particular recipe with two leftover plant-based Italian sausages. I added one of my favorite toppings, caramelized onions, and called it a day. The onions can be refrigerated and stored for future use as well.

3 medium yellow onions

2 tablespoons unsalted butter

1 tablespoon olive oil

1 tablespoon brown sugar

2 tablespoons olive oil

2 plant-based Italian sausages, sliced into bite-size pieces (half a 14-ounce package)

8 large eggs

¼ cup heavy cream

½ teaspoon salt

½ teaspoon pepper

1. To caramelize the onions, slice them thin with a mandoline or by hand.

2. In an 8″ or 10″ skillet warm the butter and olive oil on low heat. Add onions and cook for about 40 minutes, or until the onions are caramelized.

3. Stir in the brown sugar and 1 tablespoon of water. Continue to cook on low heat for another 10 minutes. Remove from heat.

4. Preheat oven to 350 degrees F.

5. In an 8″ oven-safe skillet, heat 2 tablespoons olive oil on medium heat.

6. Add the sausages and cook until browned. Keep them warm on low heat.

7. In a 1-quart mixing bowl, whisk together the eggs, cream, salt, and pepper until blended.

8. Pour the egg mixture into the skillet with the sausages and let it simmer on low for 1–2 minutes.

9. Gently place the skillet with the eggs and sausage into the oven. Bake for 10–13 minutes, or until firm and golden brown on top.

10. Remove the frittata from the oven and let it rest on the stove top. Wrap a towel around the skillet handle to remind you not to touch it.

11. Cut the frittata into triangles, like a pizza, and serve it with the caramelized onions.

12. Leftover caramelized onions can be stored in the refrigerator for up to 7 days.

Note: Be sure to use the full 2 tablespoons of olive oil when browning the sausage. This will keep the egg mixture from sticking on the skillet during the baking process.

Savory Sausage Maple Bread Pudding

SERVES 4

This is a lick-your-fingers-and-your-plate kind of recipe. Every time I make it, my family members hang out near the kitchen to try to be first in line for a helping. I typically use leftover pretzel buns or purchase pretzel bread to make this dish. The pretzel bread's softness and density allow it to soak up the egg mixture and create a creamy, rich pudding-like texture. The addition of the vegan maple sausage gives it a hint of savory and salty to complement the sweetness of the maple syrup. This recipe is a one-dish breakfast or brunch meal that will make your entire family look forward to weekends at the breakfast table.

BREAD PUDDING

6 large eggs

1 cup half-and-half

½ teaspoon salt

2 tablespoons maple syrup

5 cups pretzel buns/bread, diced into bite-size pieces

8 ounces or 1 cup of vegan maple sausage (I cut sausage into ½″ pieces)

4 tablespoons unsalted butter, divided

MAPLE BUTTER

4 tablespoons unsalted butter

2 tablespoons maple syrup

TO MAKE THE BREAD PUDDING

1. Preheat oven to 350 degrees F.

2. Using 2 tablespoons of butter, butter a 10″ x 7″ baking dish.

3. In an 8-quart mixing bowl, combine the eggs, half-and-half, salt, and maple syrup.

4. Add the pretzel buns/bread to the egg mixture.

5. Stir the bread until it's combined with the egg mixture.

6. Fold in the sausage.

7. Turn the bread, sausage, and egg mixture into the baking dish.

8. Melt 2 tablespoons of butter and pour it over the bread mixture.

9. Bake for 30 minutes, or until golden brown on top.

10. Remove from the oven. Cool for 5 minutes. While you wait for it to cool, make the maple butter.

TO MAKE THE MAPLE BUTTER

1. In a 1.5-quart saucepan, melt 4 tablespoons of butter over low heat.

2. Once melted, add 2 tablespoons of maple syrup.

3. Stir together over low heat and then remove from the heat.

4. Pour the warm maple butter over the bread pudding. Serve immediately.

Note: I used pretzel buns for the bread in this recipe, but you can substitute with a challah or brioche bread. I also recommend using real maple syrup for the highest quality maple flavor. I serve this recipe with our favorite maple syrup (for my sweets lovers) and fresh berries (for my fruit lovers).

Biscuit Breakfast Sandwich

SERVES 6

Breakfast sandwiches are at the top of our grab-and-go breakfast list. Serve them with a heaping teaspoon of jelly or honey. You can even transform them into a fun appetizer or starter for a dinner party or a girls' night in. Just substitute Brie cheese for the Havarti, fig jam for the grape jelly, and top with a few arugula leaves.

1 package refrigerated biscuit dough

12 ounces ground beef substitute

½ teaspoon salt

½ teaspoon pepper

1 teaspoon fennel seed

2 tablespoons butter, melted

2 tablespoons olive oil

6–8 slices soft cheese (I used Havarti)

Butter for spreading on biscuits

Grape, strawberry, or apricot jelly

Honey

1. Bake your favorite biscuits (6–8) according to the package instructions.

2. In a 1.5-quart mixing bowl, combine ground beef substitute, salt, pepper, fennel, and butter. Make 6 2-ounce patties. Set aside.

3. In a 10″ skillet, heat the olive oil on medium heat.

4. Cook the patties in the hot oil until the bottoms have browned. Turn the patties over and top with cheese. Continue to cook on low heat to finish cooking the patties and melt the cheese. Take each breakfast patty off the heat and place it on a paper towel–lined plate.

5. Slice the cooked biscuits in half while warm, and butter both sides. Place patties in the biscuits. Serve immediately with the jelly and honey.

Sour Cream Biscuits and Sausage Gravy

SERVES 4–6

I learned to make biscuits and gravy a very long time ago, but years later this simple recipe has stayed with me. It's the kind of comfort food my kids ask for when they're home. It even makes its way onto our family holiday menu. With easy access to plant-based meats, I can now make this for everyone in my family, and that makes everyone happy.

SOUR CREAM BISCUITS

2 cups all-purpose flour

1 tablespoon baking powder

½ teaspoon salt

1 stick cold butter cut into 6–7 pieces (2 extra tablespoons, melted)

½ cup sour cream

¾ cup whole milk

SAUSAGE GRAVY

1 7.5-ounce package vegan sausage crumbles

2 tablespoons butter

2 tablespoons all-purpose flour

2½ cups whole milk or buttermilk

¼ teaspoon red pepper flakes (optional)

TO MAKE THE BISCUITS

1. Preheat oven to 450 degrees F.

2. In a 5-quart mixing bowl, combine the flour, baking powder, and salt.

3. Add the cold butter to the flour mixture and use a fork, your hands, or a pastry blender to combine until the flour mixture is crumbly.

4. In a 3-quart mixing bowl, whisk together the sour cream and milk.

5. Add the wet ingredients to the dry ingredients a little at a time and combine in one mixing bowl.

6. Stir together until the mixture forms a soft dough.

7. Drop by spoonfuls onto a parchment-lined baking sheet.

8. Bake for 8–12 minutes, or until golden brown. When finished, brush with melted butter.

TO MAKE THE GRAVY

1. Using an 8″ skillet, cook the vegan sausage crumbles according to package directions. Turn into a bowl and set aside.

2. In the same 8″ skillet, on medium heat, melt the butter and add the flour. Whisk together until the ingredients are combined and bubbly. Turn the heat to low and slowly add the milk, whisking it into the butter-and-flour mixture.

3. Cook on low heat until the gravy begins to thicken and coats the back of your spoon. This can take 5–10 minutes.

4. Season with salt and pepper (and red pepper flakes, if desired).

5. Stir in the sausage crumbles.

6. Slice the biscuits in half, spoon the gravy over the biscuits. Serve immediately.

Note: I love to use this drop biscuit recipe for all kinds of meals. You can add cheddar cheese, garlic, and chives to create a delicious dinner biscuit as well.

Easy Breakfast Egg Muffins

SERVES 6

These savory breakfast muffins are a delicious option when you have houseguests, or just a big hungry family. The salsa adds a tangy flavor to liven up the muffins. The beef substitute and cheese make these quick-prep muffins filling and easy enough to make on a weekday morning. Serve with fresh fruit, toast, and jelly.

1 tablespoon olive oil

6 ounces ground beef substitute

½ teaspoon salt

½ teaspoon pepper

2 tablespoons butter, melted

1 cup cherry tomatoes, halved

¼ cup salsa

8 large eggs

½ cup whole milk or plain almond milk

¼ teaspoon salt

1 cup shredded cheddar cheese

1. Preheat oven to 350 degrees F.

2. Butter a 12-cup muffin pan or use cupcake liners.

3. Heat the olive oil in an 8″ skillet on medium heat.

4. Add ground beef substitute, salt, and pepper, and cook until browned.

5. Take the skillet off the heat, and add the butter, tomatoes, and salsa. Set aside.

6. In a 1.5-quart mixing bowl, whisk together the eggs, milk, and salt.

7. Fill muffin cups with the meat-and-tomato mixture. Top with the shredded cheddar.

8. Pour the egg mixture over the meat mixture and cheese, filling each muffin cup ¾ full.

9. Bake for 20–25 minutes, or until golden brown and the centers are firm.

10. Let cool for 5 minutes.

11. Serve immediately.

Note: Save yourself a step by assembling these the night before. Fill each muffin cup, cover, and refrigerate. Take the pan out 30 minutes before baking to let the mixture come to room temperature.

Pigs in a Blanket

SERVES 6

One of my favorite meals when I was a kid was *Pigs in a Blanket*. Just the thought of seeing those fluffy pancakes and savory sausage links set down in front of me makes my heart sing. And let's talk about the maple syrup—delicious, sweet, sticky goodness that makes everything come together on a plate. I've re-created this childhood favorite for my own family using vegan sausages and maple butter. I'd say this recipe makes breakfast unforgettable, one blanketed pig at a time.

1 8-ounce package vegan breakfast sausage links

1 15-ounce container whole milk ricotta cheese

1 tablespoon lemon juice

3 large eggs

¼ cup sugar

1 cup all-purpose flour

1 tablespoon baking powder

¼ teaspoon salt

2 tablespoons unsalted butter

1 cup maple syrup

1. Cook the vegan sausage links according to package instructions.

2. In a 5-quart mixing bowl, whisk together the ricotta, lemon juice, eggs, sugar, flour, baking powder, and salt.

3. Coat the bottom of a 10″ skillet with cooking spray, and warm on medium heat.

4. When the skillet is hot, add ¼ cup of batter. Spread the batter for thinner pancakes and cook for about 2 minutes or until the top is bubbling.

5. Flip the pancake and cook for another 2 minutes or until the underside is golden brown.

6. When all the pancakes are finished, place on a plate and cover.

7. In a 1.5-quart saucepan on low heat, melt the butter and add the maple syrup. Warm for about 1 minute, but do not boil.

8. To assemble *Pigs in a Blanket*, put a pancake on a plate and drizzle with the maple butter. Add 2 or 3 sausages and top with a second pancake.

9. Finish with a pat of room-temperature butter and the maple syrup.

LUNCH

Grilled Cheese Toast

SERVES 4–6

This *Grilled Cheese Toast* is such a delicious, easy to prepare lunch or light dinner. The sautéed tomatoes add a bright bruschetta feel to an already delectable open-faced sandwich. I love to make this during the tomato season when the cherry tomatoes are so sweet and velvety. The ground beef substitute makes it a more substantial meal, and the Boursin cheese gives this sandwich an herby flavor that is entirely addictive. You will want more than one!

---

4 tablespoons olive oil, divided

12 ounces ground beef substitute

½ teaspoon onion powder

½ teaspoon salt

¼ teaspoon pepper

1 pint cherry tomatoes, halved

2 garlic cloves, minced
(or 1 teaspoon minced garlic)

2 tablespoons mayonnaise

4–6 Texas toast or sourdough bread slices

½ cup Boursin cheese

4–6 cheddar cheese slices
(or 1 cup of shredded cheese)

1. In an 8″ skillet, heat 2 tablespoons of olive oil on medium heat. Add ground beef substitute, onion powder, salt, and pepper. Cook ground beef substitute until browned. Set aside.

2. In a separate 8″ skillet, heat 1 tablespoon of olive oil over medium heat.

3. Add the tomatoes and cook until the skins begin to blister. Add the garlic and continue to stir over the heat until the tomatoes soften. Be sure not to burn the garlic. Remove from the heat. Set aside.

4. Spread mayonnaise on one side of the sliced bread. Spread Boursin on the opposite side.

5. Heat the remaining olive oil in a 10″ or 12″ skillet.

6. Place the mayonnaise side of the bread in the skillet. Add the cheddar on top of the Boursin and let it warm on low heat until it begins to melt.

7. Layer on the ground beef substitute mixture and the tomatoes. Continue to warm on low heat until the bread has toasted on the bottom (about 3 minutes) and the cheddar has melted. (You can also heat the sandwiches in the oven at 350 degrees F for 5–6 minutes.)

8. Serve as an open-faced sandwich or toast.

Note: Use any flavor of Boursin cheese—they are all delicious. You can also substitute Havarti or Fontina for the cheddar.

Apple Walnut Chicken Salad

SERVES 4

There's something special about this creamy chicken salad that includes the sweetness of apples, the spice of onion, and the subtle crunch of walnuts. The other great thing about this recipe is that it works for real chicken or plant-based chicken. You can serve it over spinach for a quick lunch, or prepare it a day ahead for work and school lunches.

12 ounces or 3 cups of plant-based chicken

½ teaspoon onion powder

¾ teaspoon salt, divided

1 cup mayonnaise (vegan or regular)

¼ teaspoon pepper

2 tablespoons honey

2 teaspoons lemon juice

3 tablespoons milk

1 red apple, diced

1 red onion, diced

¼ cup walnut pieces

1. Cook the plant-based chicken according to package directions. While cooking, sprinkle with onion powder and ½ teaspoon salt. Set aside to cool.

2. In an 8-quart mixing bowl, add mayonnaise, ¼ teaspoon of salt, pepper, honey, lemon juice, and milk. Mix together well.

3. Fold in the cooled plant-based chicken, apple, onion, and walnuts.

4. Season with salt and pepper.

5. Place in an airtight container and chill for one hour.

6. Serve over salad or use in wraps or sandwiches.

Classic Patty Melt with BBQ Mayonnaise

SERVES 4

The patty melt is said to have originated in Southern California, where I grew up. I would huddle in the kitchen with my cousins around my mother and grandmother as they blanketed the patties in melted cheese and set them on buttered, toasted bread. This warm and juicy sandwich, stacked high with caramelized onions, was a little piece of heaven. I've re-created a vegetarian version of this amazing sandwich for my own family using a ground beef substitute. I use my favorite whole wheat seed bread for these patties, but they're just as delicious on rye or sourdough. The BBQ mayonnaise adds the final touch of tanginess to this comfort food.

PATTIES

12 ounces ground beef substitute

1 tablespoon Worcestershire sauce

1 teaspoon salt

½ teaspoon pepper

4 tablespoons olive oil, divided

1 medium onion, sliced thin

4 Havarti or cheddar cheese slices

2 tablespoons butter

8 whole wheat or rye bread slices

BBQ MAYONNAISE

1 teaspoon of your favorite dry BBQ seasoning

1 cup mayonnaise

½ teaspoon lemon juice

TO MAKE THE PATTIES

1. In a 5-quart mixing bowl, combine the ground beef substitute, Worcestershire sauce, salt, and pepper.

2. Make four 3-ounce patties. Set aside.

3. In a 10″ skillet, heat 2 tablespoons olive oil on medium heat.

4. Add sliced onion and cook until softened and caramelized. Put in a small bowl and cover. Set aside.

5. In the same skillet add the last 2 tablespoons of olive oil. Place patties in the skillet and cook for 2–3 minutes, until browned. Flip the patties and brown on the other side, immediately adding the cheese slices to let them melt. (Ground beef substitute cooks much faster than regular ground beef, so be sure not to overcook.)

6. Place the cooked patties on a plate and cover. Set aside

7. Melt the butter in the skillet and add the sliced bread.

8. Brown the bread on medium heat. Place on individual plates when finished.

9. Spread BBQ Mayonnaise (*recipe below*) on one slice of bread of each sandwich.

10. Top with a patty and the onions.

11. Serve immediately.

TO MAKE THE BBQ MAYONNAISE

1. Whisk all ingredients together in a small bowl.

2. Spread on toasted patty melt bread before serving. (Store up to 5 days in the refrigerator.)

Summer Corn, Tomato, and Beef Quiche

SERVES 4–6

Quiche is always in heavy rotation on my family lunch menu. It's one of those meals I can make with leftover veggies, meats, and cheese. It may sound fussy, but it's actually quick and easy. This particular recipe takes advantage of those delicious summer vegetables like tomatoes, sweet onions, and sweet corn. Adding a tasty ground beef substitute makes for a more filling meal quiche. It's 100 percent vegetarian and 0 percent guilt with a bright, fresh, and creamy taste. Get ready to add this recipe to your dinner menu rotation as well.

2 tablespoons olive oil

1 medium sweet yellow onion, diced

6 ounces ground beef substitute

1 garlic clove, minced

1 teaspoon salt, divided

1 teaspoon pepper, divided

1 15-ounce package prepared piecrust

½ cup cooked corn
(or frozen corn, thawed)

½ cup grape or cherry tomatoes,
quartered

1½ cups shredded Gruyere or
white cheddar cheese

5 large eggs

1¾ cups half-and-half or heavy cream

1 tablespoon chopped parsley

1 teaspoon chopped chives

1. Preheat oven to 350 degrees F.

2. In an 8″ skillet, heat olive oil on medium heat. Add the onion and cook for 1–2 minutes or until soft. Add the ground beef substitute, garlic, and a ½ teaspoon of both salt and pepper. Cook the ground beef substitute and onion mixture until browned. Season with salt. Set aside.

3. Roll out the piecrust and place in a pie plate or quiche dish.

4. In a 5-quart mixing bowl, combine the meat and onion mixture with the corn, tomatoes, and cheese. Toss lightly to blend together.

5. In another mixing bowl, blend the eggs, half-and-half, parsley, chives, and remaining salt and pepper.

6. Place the ground beef substitute and vegetable mixture into the piecrust, filling evenly.

7. Pour the egg mixture evenly over the meat and vegetables.

8. Bake for 30–40 minutes.

Note: I typically cut off the edge of the piecrust so it doesn't overbake in the oven. However, if you want to keep the piecrust edge, cover it with foil for the first 15–20 minutes of baking, and then remove for the remainder of the baking time.

Hot Italian Sausages with Sautéed Peppers and Onions

SERVES 4

These colorful sausage sandwiches are a favorite weekend lunch in my house, especially when everybody is cheering on their favorite teams in front of the TV. The vegan sausages are quick to cook, delicious, and filling. My crew prefers them with hot mustard, but Dijon and brown mustard are also delicious.

2 tablespoons olive oil

1 green pepper, sliced thin

1 red pepper, sliced thin

1 orange pepper, sliced thin

1 white onion, sliced thin

½ teaspoon salt

1 package vegan Italian sausages (4 in a package)

Hot mustard

4 large hot dog buns

1. In a 10″ skillet, warm the olive oil on medium heat.

2. Add the peppers and the onions to the skillet and cook for 1–2 minutes. Add ½ teaspoon of salt. Place the vegan sausages among the peppers and onions.

3. Continue to cook until the peppers and onion are soft and the vegan sausages are browned and warmed through (about 6–8 minutes).

4. Spread hot mustard on the hot dog buns, then add the sausages and cover with the peppers and onions. Serve immediately.

Note: Vegan sausages tend to dry out if overcooked. If you need to keep them moist while cooking, add ¼ cup of water.

Cheeseburger Pockets

SERVES 4-6

These *Cheeseburger Pockets* are a fun appetizer or lunch. They don't take long to prepare, which makes them an easy meal to fix, grab, and go. I like to serve these with my favorite BBQ sauce or ranch dressing. They're also tasty with the *Fun Sauce* in the *Cheeseburger Egg Roll* recipe. This is a delicious plant-based meal that even your meat lovers will appreciate. Serve with a fresh veggie platter or a salad.

12 ounces ground beef substitute

½ teaspoon salt

½ teaspoon pepper

1 teaspoon onion powder

1 small white onion, finely diced

¼ cup ketchup

¼ cup mayonnaise

3 tablespoons pickle relish (optional)

1 cup shredded Monterey Jack
or cheddar cheese

1 15-ounce package prepared piecrust

1 large egg

1 tablespoon water

1. Preheat oven to 350 degrees F.

2. In a 3-quart mixing bowl, combine ground beef substitute, salt, pepper, onion powder, onion, ketchup, mayonnaise, relish, and cheese. Mix well.

3. Roll out each piecrust with a rolling pin or your hands, spreading it about a ½ inch larger all the way around. (Two crusts come in one 15-ounce package.)

4. Cut each piecrust into quarters for a total of 8 pieces.

5. Place equal amounts of beef and cheese mixture in the middle of each piece of piecrust. Fold over to form a little pocket. Use a fork to seal the edges. Place on a parchment-lined baking sheet.

6. In a 1.5-quart mixing bowl, combine the egg and water, whisking together to make an egg wash. Using a pastry brush, cover each pocket generously with the egg wash. This will give your *Cheeseburger Pockets* a nice golden-brown color after baking.

7. Bake for 20-25 minutes. Cover with aluminum foil if the pockets brown too quickly.

Buffalo Blue Cheese Sliders

SERVES 4

I always thought someone created Buffalo sauce specifically for football season. Little did I know that it was created in 1964 by a family-owned restaurant in Buffalo, New York. Since then, Americans have been using Buffalo sauce on everything from wings to cauliflower. These *Buffalo Blue Cheese Sliders* are a huge hit with my family. Packed with flavor and topped with a crumble of blue cheese and a slathering of Buffalo aioli, they are sure to satisfy all your food cravings. For an ideal blend of flavors, serve them on a soft, slightly sweet bun, like potato rolls or Hawaiian bread.

SLIDERS

12 ounces ground beef substitute

2 tablespoons cayenne pepper hot sauce

3 tablespoons butter, divided

½ cup crumbled blue cheese, divided

2–3 tablespoons olive oil

Slider rolls

1 tomato, sliced

Lettuce leaves

BUFFALO AIOLI

½ cup mayonnaise

2 tablespoons of your favorite hot sauce (I use Frank's RedHot)

TO MAKE THE SLIDERS

1. In a 3-quart mixing bowl, combine the ground beef substitute, hot sauce, 2 tablespoons butter, and ¼ cup blue cheese, and mix well.

2. Use your hands to scoop 2–3 ounces of the mixture at a time and form small patties. Place them on parchment paper or a clean plate.

3. In a 10″ skillet, heat the olive oil. Cook the sliders on medium heat about 1–2 minutes per side. Place them on a plate and cover. (These sliders can be pink in the middle for a more tender patty.)

4. Butter the inside of the slider rolls with the remaining butter and place in the same skillet. Heat until the slider rolls become toasted.

5. Layer the patties with tomato and lettuce on the rolls. Sprinkle each with some of the remaining blue cheese.

6. Spread the aioli generously on the inside of the slider rolls before serving.

TO MAKE THE BUFFALO AIOLI

1. In a 1.5-quart mixing bowl, combine the mayonnaise and 2 tablespoons hot sauce.

Note: Serve with celery stalks and additional aioli for dipping.

Classic Sliders
with Sweet Slaw

SERVES 4

Try this plant-based lunch recipe when you want comfort food that packs a big punch in terms of flavor. These little sliders are perfectly delicious on a hot, sunny day with fresh lemonade or sangria. They're also as easy to make on a grill as they are on the stove top. Try a sweet slider roll for added flavor.

SWEET SLAW

¾ cup mayonnaise

¼ cup milk

½ teaspoon salt

¼ teaspoon pepper

1 tablespoon rice wine vinegar

1½ tablespoons honey

1 10-ounce package finely shredded green cabbage

SLIDERS

12 ounces ground beef substitute

½ teaspoon onion powder

½ teaspoon garlic powder

¼ teaspoon salt

¼ teaspoon pepper

¼ teaspoon allspice

1–2 tablespoons olive oil

2 tablespoons butter

4 slider rolls

2 Roma tomatoes, sliced thin

1 red onion, sliced thin

TO MAKE THE SWEET SLAW

1. In a 3-quart mixing bowl, whisk together the mayonnaise, milk, salt, pepper, vinegar, and honey.

2. Fold in shredded cabbage and refrigerate for 30 minutes.

TO MAKE THE SLIDERS

1. In a 3-quart mixing bowl, combine the ground beef substitute, onion powder, garlic powder, salt, pepper, and allspice.

2. Use your hands to scoop 2–3 ounces of the mixture at a time and form small patties. Place them on parchment paper or a clean plate.

3. In a 10″ skillet, warm the olive oil. Cook the sliders on medium heat about 1–2 minutes per side. Place them on a plate and cover. (These sliders can be pink in the middle for a more tender patty.)

4. Butter the inside of the slider rolls and place in the same skillet. Heat until they are toasted.

5. Place the patties on the rolls and layer the patties with tomato, onion, and a spoonful of slaw.

6. Serve immediately.

Note: You can serve with condiments, but the slaw is extremely creamy and ample on its own.

APPETIZERS

Arancini
with Spicy Marinara

SERVES 4–6

Arancini (or Italian Rice Balls) are an Italian street vendor specialty. This dish has gained popularity in the United States, where it is commonly found on the menus of both upscale and small, family-run Italian restaurants. You can create this cheesy, plant-based version in your own home with a starchy, short-grain rice called arborio rice. The process begins with a delicious risotto and ends with a spicy marinara sauce. It's sure to please both meat eaters and vegetarians, and can be served as an appetizer or a meal.

---

3 cups vegetable stock

1 teaspoon salt, divided

1 cup arborio rice

1 tablespoon olive oil

6 ounces ground beef substitute

¼ teaspoon onion powder

2 large eggs

⅓ cup shredded Parmesan cheese

1 cup seasoned Italian bread crumbs, divided

1 cup diced Fontina cheese

Vegetable oil

Marinara sauce

¼ teaspoon red pepper flakes

Grated Parmesan cheese for garnish

1. In a 3-quart saucepan, heat the vegetable stock and ½ teaspoon of salt.

2. Bring the vegetable stock to a boil, add rice, cover and simmer on low for 18–22 minutes. When the rice is finished cooking, spread it on a parchment-lined baking sheet to cool.

3. In an 8″ skillet, heat the olive oil on medium heat. Add the ground beef substitute, remaining salt, and the onion powder. Cook until browned. Set aside.

4. In a 1.5-quart mixing bowl, combine the ground beef substitute mixture, rice, eggs, Parmesan, and ½ cup of the Italian bread crumbs.

5. Use your hands to scoop a little of the mixture at a time and form fifteen 1.5″ rice balls. Place them on the baking sheet.

6. Use your finger to poke a hole into the center of each rice ball, and fill it with Fontina. Roll the rice balls in the remaining Italian bread crumbs and place them back on the baking sheet.

7. Heat the vegetable oil to around 365 degrees F in a large stockpot. Use enough oil to cover the rice balls.

8. Using tongs, place 3–4 balls in the hot oil. Cook until golden brown. Remove the rice balls as they cook and place them back on the baking sheet.

9. In a 1.5-quart saucepan heat your favorite marinara sauce until warm and steamy. Add the red pepper flakes.

10. Serve arancini with a side of the spicy marinara. Sprinkle with Parmesan.

Note: You can make the rice a day ahead and store it in the fridge. Let it come to room temperature before making the rice balls.

Poutine

SERVES 4–6

This *Poutine* recipe is a delicious spin on the popular Canadian dish of French fries and cheese curds covered in gravy. I use baby potatoes instead, and layer on a quick sauce and a lot of gooey cheese. My version is baked, not fried, so the potatoes have a roasted flavor that complements the gravy. Eat with your fingers or a fork—it all works, and it's delicious!

GRAVY

1 tablespoon olive oil

12 ounces ground beef substitute

½ teaspoon garlic powder

¼ teaspoon smoked paprika

1 teaspoon pepper, divided

1 teaspoon flake or kosher salt, divided

4 tablespoons unsalted butter

¼ cup all-purpose flour

2 cups vegetable stock

¼ cup whole milk

POUTINE

24 ounces Baby Dutch yellow potatoes

2 tablespoons olive oil

¼ teaspoon pepper

½ teaspoon flake or kosher salt

1½ cups shredded cheddar cheese

¼ cup diced red onion (for garnish)

¼ cup chopped green onion (for garnish)

TO MAKE THE BEEF GRAVY

1. In a 10″ skillet, add 1 tablespoon of olive oil, ground beef substitute, garlic powder, smoked paprika, ½ teaspoon pepper, and ½ teaspoon salt. Cook on medium heat, separating into crumbles with a wooden spoon until it's fully browned. Pour cooked ground beef substitute into a bowl and set aside.

2. Using the same 10″ skillet, melt the butter over medium heat. When the butter is melted and begins to darken in color, add the flour and stir for about 3 minutes to create the roux for the gravy.

3. Once the flour and butter are a golden brown, turn the heat to low and slowly add the vegetable stock and milk while whisking quickly. Continue to whisk until the gravy thickens and forms a coating on the back of a spoon. Stir in ½ teaspoon of the flake salt (or kosher salt) and ½ teaspoon pepper.

4. Add the ground beef substitute to the gravy mixture. Season with salt and pepper. Set aside.

TO MAKE THE POUTINE

1. Preheat oven to 425 degrees F.

2. Slice the baby potatoes into quarters in a uniform size to cook evenly.

3. In a 5-quart mixing bowl, toss the potatoes with the olive oil, pepper, and ½ teaspoon flake or kosher salt.

4. Layer the potatoes evenly on a parchment-lined baking sheet and place in the oven for 15–17 minutes.

5. When the potatoes are finished, turn the oven down to 350 degrees F.

6. Spoon ¼ of the gravy mixture into the bottom of a 9" x 12" casserole dish.

7. Layer ½ of the roasted potatoes over the gravy and add ½ of the cheddar cheese over the potatoes. Add the remaining potatoes followed by the remaining gravy. Top with the rest of the cheddar cheese.

8. Place the casserole dish in the oven for 10 minutes, or until the top layer of the cheese is bubbly and golden brown.

9. When finished, garnish with the red onion and the green onion.

Note: If you are short on vegetable stock, substitute 1 cup of beer and 1 cup of vegetable stock, or use beef broth.

Weekend Nachos Topped with Elote

SERVES 3–4

My family is crazy about these *Weekend Nachos*, and who doesn't love elote—that creamy, spicy street corn that is a staple side dish in many households? I combined these two delectable weekend dishes into one fabulous meal. I used a pre-crumbled and spiced, plant-based meat substitute, but you can substitute your favorite plant-based protein. With a mix of textures and loads of flavor, these nachos make a satisfying appetizer, weekday meal, or late-night snack. If time is of the essence, you can leave out the elote, but if you have time to include it, you'll discover that it's worth the extra steps.

ELOTE

4 ears fresh corn (washed),
or about 10 ounces cooked corn

½ cup mayonnaise

Juice from 1 lime

1½ teaspoons Tajin seasoning

½ cup crumbled cotija cheese

WEEKEND NACHOS

1 tablespoon vegetable oil

10 ounces plant-based meat crumbles
(mine were spiced with taco seasoning)

½ teaspoon cumin

1 teaspoon garlic powder

½ teaspoon salt

1 15.5-ounce can chili beans or
black beans in chili sauce

¼ cup finely chopped cilantro

¼ cup water

1 9-ounce bag tortilla chips

2 cups shredded cheddar cheese,
divided

1 cup halved grape tomatoes

½ cup halved or sliced black olives

½ cup diced red onion

1 avocado, diced

¼ cup chopped green onions

TO MAKE THE ELOTE

1. On an outdoor grill or in a 10″ skillet, cook the corn (on the cob) over medium heat for 4–6 minutes. (It's finished when grill marks form on the corn. If the corn overcooks, it will be chewy or soggy.) Set aside. **Note:** If you're using pre-cooked corn, simply heat it up in the skillet.

2. While the corn is cooling, whisk together the mayonnaise, lime juice, and Tajin seasoning in a 3-quart mixing bowl.

3. Gently fold in the crumbled cotija.

4. Cut the corn off the cobs and add the kernels to the mayonnaise and lime juice mixture. (It should be creamy.)

TO MAKE THE NACHOS

1. Preheat oven to 350 degrees F.

2. In a 9″ sauté pan, warm the vegetable oil on medium heat.

3. Add the plant-based meat crumbles and cook on medium low heat.

4. Stir in the cumin, garlic powder, and salt.

5. Add the chili beans or black beans, stirring slowly to prevent burning.

6. Gently stir in the cilantro and water, and cook for about 2 minutes, or until the meat crumbles mixture is nice and creamy. Do not overcook.

7. Take the meat crumbles and bean mixture off the heat. Set aside.

8. Place ½ of the tortilla chips on a parchment-lined baking sheet and sprinkle with 1 cup of the cheddar.

9. Gently pour the meat crumbles and bean mixture over the tortilla chips, and sprinkle on the remaining cheddar.

10. Bake for 8 minutes, or until the chips darken and the cheese melts.

11. When cheese is melted, remove the baking sheet from the oven and top the nachos with the tomatoes, black olives, red onion, and avocado.

12. Finish by spooning on the elote and garnishing with the green onions.

Beef and Corn Fritters with Jalapeño Lime Crema

SERVES 4

I would seriously fritter everything if I could. I crave the crispy texture of the outer layer of the fritter combined with the fluffy pancake-like center. And when you take that first bite, it all comes together as one amazing burst of texture and flavor. These ground beef substitute and corn fritters are all that and more. They're a delicious, hearty meal on their own or an excellent starter. I serve these with honey and *Jalapeño Lime Crema* to add a spicy-sweet element to the recipe.

FRITTERS

1 tablespoon olive oil

6 ounces ground beef substitute

½ teaspoon cumin

1 teaspoon salt, divided

2 cups corn

1 cup all-purpose flour

1 teaspoon baking powder

1 cup half-and-half (or whole milk)

2 large eggs

¼ cup chopped cilantro

½ teaspoon pepper

1½ tablespoons honey

Oil for frying (I used olive oil, but vegetable oil also works)

JALAPEÑO LIME CREMA

1 cup sour cream

1 jalapeño pepper, seeded and diced

1 tablespoon lime juice

1 teaspoon lime zest

TO MAKE THE FRITTERS

1. In an 8″ skillet, heat the olive oil on medium heat. Add the ground beef substitute, cumin, and ¼ teaspoon salt. Cook the ground beef substitute until browned. Set aside.

2. In a 5-quart mixing bowl, add the ground beef substitute mixture, corn, flour, baking powder, half-and-half, eggs, cilantro, remaining salt, pepper, and honey. Mix well. The mixture will be thick.

3. In a 10″ skillet, add a ¼–½″ layer of olive or vegetable oil. Heat oil on medium high heat.

4. Drop the ground beef substitute and corn mixture by the tablespoon into the hot oil, and cook until the fritters are golden brown on each side (2–3 minutes). Place on a paper towel–lined plate. Repeat until the mixture is gone.

5. Top fritters with *Jalapeño Lime Crema* (recipe below) and a drizzle of honey.

TO MAKE THE JALAPEÑO LIME CREMA

1. In a 1.5-quart mixing bowl, combine the sour cream, jalapeño, lime juice, lime zest, and season with salt. Mix well.

Note: I used grilled corn (4 corn cobs rendered 2 cups of corn), but you can use frozen corn that has thawed. I would not recommend canned corn.

Party Meatballs

SERVES 4–6

These *Party Meatballs* are one of those traditional party appetizers I've always made with regular ground beef. Now I can make them fully vegetarian. I've also added two party sauce options. I'm certain that you can purchase ready-made plant-based meatballs, but they'll taste better if you make them with your own ingredients. You can always freeze them for future parties, too!

MEATBALLS

12 ounces ground beef substitute

½ teaspoon salt

¼ teaspoon pepper

1 garlic clove, minced

¼ teaspoon ground allspice

¼ cup bread crumbs (softened with a tablespoon of milk)

1 large egg

PARTY SAUCE #1

1 cup barbecue sauce

¾ cup grape jelly

PARTY SAUCE #2

½ cup sweet chili sauce

⅓ cup fig preserves

TO MAKE THE MEATBALLS

1. Preheat oven to 350 degrees F.

2. In a 3-quart mixing bowl, combine the ground beef substitute, salt, pepper, garlic, allspice, bread crumbs, and egg.

3. Use your hands to scoop a little of the mixture at a time and form 15 small meatballs. Place them on a parchment-lined baking sheet.

4. Bake for 20 minutes.

5. In a 4-quart saucepan, combine the ingredients for one of the two sauces, and warm on low heat until simmering.

6. Drop the cooked meatballs into the sauce and simmer for about 5 minutes until meatballs are coated. Serve warm.

Note: The meatballs (without the sauce) can be frozen for several months.

Tater Tot Nachos with Cheese Sauce

SERVES 4–6

These *Tater Tot Nachos* make a fun and delicious snack or appetizer. Add plant-based beef and you've also got a quick, easy meal! I make my own cheese sauce, but you can purchase a sauce if time is an issue. I've also made this with vegetable tots, typically available in the frozen vegetable section of the grocery store.

CHEESE SAUCE

4 tablespoons butter

4 tablespoons all-purpose flour

2 cups whole milk, room temperature

4 cups shredded cheddar cheese
(or pepper jack cheese to make it spicy)

TATER TOT NACHOS

1 28-ounce bag frozen Tater Tots
(or veggie tots)

4 tablespoons olive oil

2–3 Anaheim peppers, sliced

2–3 hot chili peppers, sliced

12 ounces ground beef substitute

½ teaspoon salt

½ teaspoon pepper

2 garlic cloves, minced

1 red onion, diced

1 avocado, diced

TO MAKE THE CHEESE SAUCE

1. In a 10″ skillet, melt the butter over medium heat.

2. Once the butter has melted, add the flour and stir together for about 1 minute.

3. Turn to low heat and slowly add the milk to the butter and flour mixture, stirring quickly to combine and make a roux. Continue stirring until the mixture thickens and coats the back of a spoon.

4. Remove from the heat and immediately stir in the cheese until melted. Season with salt and pepper.

TO MAKE THE TATER TOT NACHOS

1. Preheat oven to 425 degrees F.

2. Bake the Tater Tots according to package directions. Season with salt. Set aside.

3. In an 8″ skillet, heat the olive oil on medium high heat. Add all of the peppers and cook until they begin to brown and look a little crisp. Remove when browned and place on a paper towel–lined plate.

4. In the same skillet on medium heat, add the ground beef substitute, salt, pepper, and garlic. Cook until browned.

5. Place the Tater Tots in a serving dish and cover with the cooked ground beef substitute. Layer on the cheese sauce.

6. Sprinkle the peppers, red onion, and avocado on top. Serve immediately.

Note: I use the extra cheese sauce for individual dipping bowls. Leftover cheese sauce can be refrigerated and stored for up to 4 days.

Spicy Cheesy Chili Dip

SERVES 4

I love the smoky, spicy taste of chipotle peppers. When I created this recipe, I was excited to find a way to incorporate their unique flavor into the dip. You can use canned chipotle peppers in adobo sauce for this recipe. I keep a can of pureed peppers in my refrigerator for meals just like this one. Serve with your favorite tortilla chips for a fun starter!

2 tablespoons olive oil

12 ounces ground beef substitute

2 teaspoons minced garlic

½ cup chipotle peppers in adobo sauce (pureed or finely chopped)

1 cup cream cheese, softened

1 15.5-ounce can black beans or kidney beans, drained and rinsed

1½ cups finely shredded cheddar cheese

1 cup sour cream

1 red onion, diced

½ cup pickled jalapeño peppers

Tortilla chips for serving

1. Preheat oven to 375 degrees F.

2. In an 8″ skillet, heat the olive oil on medium heat. Add the ground beef substitute, garlic, and chipotles. Stir together and cook until the ground beef substitute has browned.

3. Remove from the heat and immediately stir in the cream cheese until melted.

4. Add the beans to the ground beef substitute mixture. Mix well.

5. Place ⅓ of the mixture in the bottom of an 8″ x 8″ baking dish.

6. Layer ⅓ of the cheddar over the mixture.

7. Continue layering, with 3 layers of ground beef substitute mixture and 3 layers of cheese.

8. Bake for 20–25 minutes, or until golden brown on top and bubbly on the sides.

9. Cool for 5 minutes. Top with the sour cream. Sprinkle diced onion and jalapeño over the sour cream.

10. Serve with tortilla chips.

Beefy Cheddar Bites

SERVES 4–6

These *Beefy Cheddar Bites* make a fantastic quick and easy snack for that last-minute football party or when friends drop by for an unexpected visit. They are unbelievably easy to make and will satisfy all of your snack food cravings. The soft, cheesy morsels pair well with your favorite beer or spirits and good friends.

1 cup pancake or biscuit mix

6 ounces ground beef substitute

1 cup shredded cheddar cheese

1 tablespoon mayonnaise

2 teaspoons dry ranch dressing mix

1. Preheat oven to 400 degrees F.

2. In an 8-quart mixing bowl, combine the biscuit mix, ground beef substitute, cheddar, mayonnaise, and ranch dressing mix.

3. Use your hands to scoop a little of the mixture at a time and form small balls. Place them on a parchment-lined baking sheet about 1″ apart. Repeat until the mixture is gone.

4. Bake for 10–13 minutes.

5. Remove from oven and serve.

Pizza Dip

SERVES 4–6

Pizza is always a good idea, but *Pizza Dip* is an even better one! This is an easy starter to prepare and serve. It's one of my favorites because it goes from the stove to the oven to the table in one pan. Add your favorite crusty bread and you've got a warm, gooey, cheesy snack that everyone will enjoy.

1 tablespoon olive oil

8 ounces ground beef substitute

2 garlic cloves, diced

½ teaspoon salt

½ teaspoon pepper

1 teaspoon Italian seasoning

8 ounces cream cheese, cubed, room temperature

1½ cups pizza sauce (or *Sunday Sauce*, see page 76)

½ cup shredded Parmesan cheese

2 cups shredded mozzarella cheese

¼ cup sliced black olives

½ red onion, sliced

1. Preheat oven to 375 degrees F.

2. In an 8″, oven proof skillet, heat the olive oil on medium heat.

3. Add the ground beef substitute, garlic, salt, pepper, and Italian seasoning. Stir together and cook until the ground beef substitute has browned.

4. Remove from the heat and immediately stir in the cream cheese until melted.

5. Add the pizza sauce.

6. Sprinkle the Parmesan and mozzarella over the ground beef substitute and cheese mixture.

7. Top with the black olives and onion.

8. Bake for 20 minutes, or until bubbly and golden brown on top.

9. Cool for 5 minutes. Serve with crusty bread or pita chips.

Note: Feel free to get creative with the toppings by adding jalapeño, sweet peppers, or sun-dried tomatoes.

Beef Cheese Puffs with Honey Mustard Sauce

SERVES 6

These light and fluffy *Beef Cheese Puffs* are melt-in-your-mouth delicious. This recipe's base is a classic pâte à choux dough. When you combine it with cheese and beef, it makes a fun appetizer for any event or dinner party. This recipe is so easy, you will find yourself turning to it again and again. You can substitute the cheddar cheese with almost any firm cheese, and if you want to change the herbs, try dried oregano or rosemary.

BEEF CHEESE PUFFS

1 tablespoon olive oil

6 ounces ground beef substitute

¾ teaspoon salt, divided

¼ teaspoon pepper

¼ teaspoon minced garlic

1 cup water

8 tablespoons cold, unsalted butter, cut into pieces

1 cup all-purpose flour

4 large eggs, room temperature

1½ cups shredded cheddar cheese

1 teaspoon dried parsley

1 teaspoon dried chives

HONEY MUSTARD SAUCE

¼ cup honey

¼ cup yellow mustard

3 tablespoons mayonnaise

½ tablespoon lemon juice

TO MAKE THE PUFFS

1. Preheat oven to 400 degrees F.

2. In an 8″ skillet, heat the olive oil on medium heat. Add the ground beef substitute, ¼ teaspoon salt, pepper, and garlic. Stir together and cook until the ground beef substitute has browned. Set aside.

3. In a 5-quart saucepan, heat water, butter, and ½ teaspoon salt on medium high heat. Bring to a boil.

4. Add the flour and stir quickly. Reduce the heat to medium low and continue to stir until the mixture begins to pull away from the sides of the saucepan.

5. Remove from the heat and cool for 1 minute. Slowly add eggs, one at a time. Mix as you add each egg.

6. Fold in the cheddar, parsley, chives, and ground beef substitute.

7. Use a tablespoon to form small dough balls. Place each on a parchment-lined baking sheet.

8. Bake for 8–10 minutes. Lower the heat to 350 degrees F. Bake for another 20 minutes, or until golden brown.

TO MAKE THE HONEY MUSTARD SAUCE

1. In a 1.5-quart mixing bowl, add honey, mustard, mayonnaise, and lemon juice. Blend together with a small whisk or fork.

Cheeseburger Egg Rolls with Fun Sauce

SERVES 4

I first created these *Cheeseburger Egg Rolls* for a movie night. They were gobbled up so fast that I doubled the recipe the next time. I recommend using your favorite hamburger or grill seasoning to keep this recipe quick and easy. I created the *Fun Sauce* after tasting a special sauce at one of my favorite burger stands. I don't think this is the exact taste, but it's close, and my family loves it.

FUN SAUCE

¼ cup mayonnaise

¼ cup ketchup

1 tablespoon pickle relish

¼ teaspoon garlic powder

⅛ teaspoon paprika

¼ teaspoon Sriracha sauce (optional)

EGG ROLLS

12 ounces ground beef substitute

2 teaspoons hamburger seasoning

2 tablespoons olive oil

1 small onion, diced

1 package egg roll wrappers (7" x 7" works best)

½ cup water

1½ cups shredded cheddar cheese

Vegetable oil for frying

Pickles for garnish

TO MAKE THE FUN SAUCE

1. In a 1.5-quart mixing bowl, combine mayonnaise, ketchup, pickle relish, garlic powder, paprika, and Sriracha, if using.

2. Mix together, and chill for 15–20 minutes.

TO MAKE THE EGG ROLLS

1. In a 1.5-quart mixing bowl, combine the ground beef substitute and hamburger seasoning.

2. In an 8" skillet, heat the olive oil on medium heat. Add the onion and cook until translucent.

3. Add the ground beef substitute. Stir together and cook until the ground beef substitute has browned. Set aside.

4. Brush the edges of the egg roll wrappers with the water. Fill one end of the wrapper with equal parts ground beef substitute mixture and cheddar.

5. Gently roll the wrapper over once and fold in the sides. Continue to roll and seal the edges with water. Place each finished egg roll on a parchment-lined baking sheet.

6. In an 8- or 10-quart stockpot, heat the vegetable oil. Use just enough to cover the egg rolls when they are placed in the hot oil.

7. Use tongs to place a few egg rolls at a time in the hot oil after it reaches 365 degrees F. Turn the egg rolls when they reach a toasty brown color. Once all sides are browned, remove them from the hot oil and place on the parchment-lined baking sheet.

8. Cut the egg rolls in half and serve with chilled *Fun Sauce* and the pickles.

Stuffed Mushrooms

SERVES 4

Like many people, I haven't always had a fondness for mushrooms. Today I completely adore their earthy flavor and luscious texture. They're also a great source of fiber, potassium, B vitamins, and antioxidants. I hesitated to make stuffed mushrooms until I discovered plant-based ground beef products. Most vegetarian recipes include a lot of bread crumbs and other fillers. Here I've used the mushroom stem along with a ground beef substitute to create a tasty filling that pops with flavor and satisfies. These are hearty enough to turn into a meal!

16 ounces organic whole baby bello mushrooms or baby portobello mushrooms (substitute 2 large portobello mushrooms)

1½ tablespoons olive oil

6–8 ounces ground beef substitute

3 garlic cloves, minced

1 teaspoon dried oregano

½ teaspoon salt

½ teaspoon pepper

⅓ cup Boursin shallot and chive cheese

½ cup finely shredded mozzarella cheese, plus 3 tablespoons for topping

Ranch dressing, for dipping

1. Preheat oven to 350 degrees F.

2. Rinse the mushrooms well.

3. Remove the stems and dice them into small pieces. Set aside.

4. Use a small spoon or a butter knife to take out the gills under the cap to make space for the filling.

5. In an 8″ skillet heat the olive oil on medium heat.

6. Add the ground beef substitute, garlic, oregano, salt, and pepper. Stir together and cook until the ground beef substitute has browned.

7. In a 3-quart mixing bowl, combine the ground beef substitute mixture and the diced mushroom stems. Mix in the Boursin and mozzarella. Season with salt.

8. Use a small spoon to fill the mushroom caps with the ground beef substitute and the diced mushroom stems mixture. Place the caps on a parchment-lined baking sheet. Sprinkle on the mozzarella.

9. Bake for 15–20 minutes, or until golden brown and the cheese has melted.

10. Serve with a side of ranch dressing for dipping.

DINNER

The Backyard Burger

SERVES 3–4

My family looks forward to those evenings or weekends when we grill up all of our favorites, especially these big, juicy burgers. With a vegetarian in the family, and a few of us who would prefer an occasional plant-based option, *The Backyard Burger* is the perfect solution. You can make them on the grill or in a skillet. Add additional flavor by buttering the hamburger buns and placing on your skillet to lightly toast just before serving. It gives the bread a nice crisp texture and buttery flavor that complements the plant-based meat substitute. Layer on fresh toppings and creamy ranch dressing to take these satisfying, beef-free burgers to the next level. This recipe makes three 4-ounce burgers or four 3-ounce burgers. Enjoy!

12 ounces ground beef substitute

½ teaspoon chipotle chili powder (or regular chili powder)

1 teaspoon garlic powder

½ teaspoon onion powder

½ teaspoon paprika

½ teaspoon salt

¼ teaspoon pepper

½ cup olive oil

4 cheddar cheese slices

4 hamburger buns

Large lettuce leaves

1 tomato, sliced

1 red onion, sliced

Pickles

Ranch dressing

1. In a 5-quart mixing bowl, add the ground beef substitute, chili powder, garlic powder, onion powder, paprika, salt, and pepper. Use your hands to mix well.

2. Make hamburger patties. Set aside.

3. In a 10"–12" skillet, warm olive oil on medium heat. The patties will brown quickly, so be sure the heat is not too high. If you prefer to use a grill, see the note below.

4. Place the patties in the skillet and cook for 3–4 minutes on each side. The patties can be cooked to individual preference but are generally moister with a little pink in the middle.

5. Melt the cheese on the patties a few minutes before completely cooked.

6. Place patties on the buns, and top with the lettuce, tomato, onion, pickles, and ranch dressing.

Note: Before cooking the patties on a conventional grill, spray a large piece of aluminum foil with cooking spray and poke a few small holes in the foil. Place the foil on the grill and place the patties on the foil.

Beef Enchiladas

SERVES 4–6

I grew up in Southern California where there's plenty of Mexican cuisine and influences. Our family meals included Baja fish tacos, sopes, and crispy corn-rolled tacos filled with shredded beef and heaped with fresh guacamole and tomatoes. Saturdays for my family meant carne asada burritos and a trip to the beach. When I began my quest to make meat-free Mexican food that didn't take a half day to prepare, I looked for ingredients that were quick and easy, and bursting with SoCal flavor. When I added a ground beef substitute to this recipe, I was happy to discover that the wow factor still remained. These warm, cheesy, *Beef Enchiladas* are my delicious tribute to my SoCal roots.

1 8-ounce package plain white or cilantro lime rice

1 tablespoon olive oil

1 medium onion, diced

12 ounces ground beef substitute

½ teaspoon chipotle chili powder (or regular chili powder)

½ teaspoon salt

1 cup black beans in chili sauce

1 10-ounce can diced tomatoes with green chilies (mild or hot)

3 cups enchilada sauce, divided

1 cup sliced black olives

6–8 flour tortillas

2 cups pepper jack cheese or Monterey Jack (for less spice)

1 cup sour cream

¼ cup chopped green onions

1 avocado, diced

¼ cup chopped red onion

1. Preheat oven to 350 degrees F.

2. Cook rice according to package instructions. Set aside.

3. In a 10″ skillet, heat oil on medium heat.

4. Add the onion and cook until caramelized.

5. Add the ground beef substitute, chili powder, and salt. Cook until browned.

6. Add the black beans, tomatoes, and 1½ cups of the enchilada sauce. Stir together and simmer on low heat for about 3 minutes.

7. Add the black olives. Remove from the heat. Set aside.

8. Use a spatula to cover the bottom of an 11″ x 8″ or 9″ x 13″ baking dish with 2–3 tablespoons of the remaining enchilada sauce.

9. Fill each tortilla with 2 tablespoons of the ground beef substitute mixture, 1 tablespoon of rice, and ½ tablespoon of shredded cheese. Roll each tortilla and place seam-side down into the baking dish. There should be 6–8 enchiladas.

10. Pour the remaining sauce over the enchiladas and sprinkle with the remaining cheese.

11. Cover the baking dish with foil and place in the oven. Cook for 15 minutes. Take foil off and cook for another 10–15 minutes or until the top is bubbly and golden brown. If the top is not browning, turn the oven to broil and cook for about 3 minutes.

12. Remove the baking dish and let the enchiladas rest for 10 minutes before serving.

13. Garnish with sour cream, green onions, avocado, and red onion.

Note: These enchiladas are delicious served with a side of *Elote* (see page 48).

Cajun Beef and Cheesy Grits

SERVES 6

Laissez les bons temps rouler! You will be feeling those good times roll with this *Cajun Beef and Cheesy Grits* recipe. It's comfort food with a vegetarian twist. I love making this dish because it's so versatile, full of flavor, and made by using what you have on hand. For example, I use white cheddar cheese, but you can also try Gruyere or Swiss. The ground beef substitute adds amazing texture, and the vegetables are chunky and al dente, allowing for a lighter version of the more traditional shrimp and grits dish. Serve family style or in individual pasta bowls. Double the recipe for larger groups or for leftovers.

CHEESY GRITS

2½ cups whole milk

2 tablespoons butter

½ cup 5-minute grits

1 cup shredded cheddar cheese

CAJUN BEEF

1 tablespoon olive oil

12 ounces ground beef substitute

2 teaspoons Cajun seasoning*

2 garlic cloves, minced

½ teaspoon salt

1 sweet onion, chopped in large pieces

1 red onion, chopped in large pieces

1–2 medium jalapeño peppers, seeded and diced (the seeds make it spicy)

1 zucchini, quartered

1½ cups sliced mushrooms

1 cup vegetable stock

1 cup grape tomatoes, halved

Crème fraîche or sour cream (optional)

TO MAKE THE GRITS

1. In a 5-quart saucepan, heat the milk and butter on medium heat. Bring to a simmer. (A roaring boil will scorch the milk on the bottom of the pan.)

2. Add the grits. Stir quickly to mix.

3. Remove from the heat when the grits thicken. Add the cheese. Season with salt and pepper. Cover and set aside.

TO MAKE THE BEEF

1. In a 10″ skillet, heat the olive oil on medium heat. Add the ground beef substitute, Cajun seasoning, and the garlic. Cook for 4 minutes, or until browned.

2. Add the salt, onions, jalapeños, zucchini, mushrooms, and vegetable stock.

3. Simmer the mixture for about 5 minutes. Add tomatoes, and salt and pepper, if needed. (The vegetables should be al dente.)

4. If you prefer a stronger Cajun seasoning, add ½ teaspoon to the final mixture.

5. Place the cheesy grits in a pasta bowl and top with the *Cajun Beef* mixture. Dollop with crème fraîche or sour cream, if desired.

*Note: If you don't have Cajun seasoning, substitute with Lawry's seasoned salt, 1 teaspoon of pepper, and 1 teaspoon of brown sugar. You can also substitute the cheddar cheese with Swiss or Gruyere cheese.

Italian Meatballs with Quick Sunday Sauce

SERVES 4–6

Italian Meatballs with Quick Sunday Sauce is a staple weekend meal in our house. This version is a bit different because it's created specifically for a beef substitute. You'll notice that I didn't use milk (typically in a meatball recipe), and I've increased the amount of bread crumbs to keep the meatballs firm, but not dry. The *Quick Sunday Sauce* is one of my favorites as well. You can use this sauce recipe for just about any Italian dish, but it's especially delicious on meatballs.

Note: If you're making the *Quick Sunday Sauce* recipe for this dish, prepare the sauce first and let it simmer while you prepare the meatballs.

QUICK SUNDAY SAUCE

1 12-ounce can whole San Marzano tomatoes

1 tablespoon garlic powder

½ tablespoon dried parsley

½ tablespoon dried basil

1 teaspoon kosher salt

1 tablespoon white sugar

1 tablespoon tomato paste

½ cup red wine

½ cup water (use pasta water when possible)

ITALIAN MEATBALLS

16 ounces ground beef substitute

1 tablespoon garlic powder

1 clove garlic, minced

1 teaspoon ground fennel seed (or ground caraway seed)

1½ tablespoons dried parsley

1½ tablespoons dried basil

1 teaspoon pepper

½ teaspoon salt

⅓ cup seasoned panko bread crumbs

⅓ cup shredded Parmesan cheese, plus more for garnish

2 large eggs, slightly beaten

½ cup olive oil

16 ounces spaghetti or angel hair pasta

¼ cup chopped parsley for garnish

TO MAKE THE SAUCE

1. In a 12″ mixing bowl, add the tomatoes and crush them with your hands until broken into small chunks.

2. Add the garlic powder, parsley, basil, salt, and sugar. Combine until blended.

3. In a 10″ saucepan, heat the tomato mixture on medium heat. Stir in the tomato paste, red wine, and water. Cover.

4. Let the sauce simmer for 30 minutes or while cooking your meatballs.

TO MAKE THE MEATBALLS

1. In a 10″ mixing bowl, add the ground beef substitute.

2. Add the next 10 ingredients. Combine using your hands to mix.

3. Use your hands to scoop a little of the mixture at a time and form meatballs. Place them on a parchment-lined baking sheet.

4. In a 10″ or 12″ saucepan, heat the olive oil on medium heat.

5. Drop each meatball into the saucepan. Brown on all sides. This will take 3–4 minutes. (Meatballs will be very soft at this point.)

6. Remove from the heat. Cover. Set aside.

7. Cook pasta according to the package instructions, and transfer it to a mixing bowl.

8. Toss the pasta with ½ the sauce. Divide into bowls and top each with meatballs.

9. Spoon the remaining sauce over the meatballs and garnish with parsley and Parmesan.

Mini Beef Pot Pies

SERVES 3 (5" PIES)–6 (3" MINI PIES)

When I think of comfort food, I think of this recipe. It's also an opportunity to use any fun, colorful ramekins you may have for individual pies. To make this recipe a bit more time friendly, I use prepared piecrust and a package of organic frozen vegetables. Never feel bad about using these shortcuts; it's all about getting everyone to the table to enjoy good food and family time. I serve these pot pies with a side of sliced tomatoes drizzled with extra virgin olive oil, a squeeze of lemon juice, and a sprinkle of salt and pepper.

---

1 package prepared piecrust (2 rolls)

2 tablespoons olive oil

1 medium yellow onion, diced

1½ cups diced potatoes

12 ounces ground beef substitute

2 garlic cloves, minced

2 teaspoons salt, divided

2 teaspoons pepper, divided

½ teaspoon dried sage
(or 1 teaspoon chopped fresh sage)

1 teaspoon Worcestershire sauce

⅔ cup frozen mixed vegetables
(carrots, peas, corn, and green beans)

6 tablespoons unsalted butter

¼ cup flour

1 cup whole milk or half-and-half,
room temperature

1½ cups vegetable stock

1 large egg

2 tablespoons water

1. Preheat oven to 350 degrees F.

2. Spray the ramekins with cooking spray.

3. Roll out the prepared piecrust and cut it into three pieces. Use each piece as the base, and mold the crust to the sides of the ramekin. Save the second piecrust for the tops.

4. In a 10″ sauté pan, heat the olive oil on medium heat. Add the onion. Cook until warmed (it does not need to be translucent).

5. Add the potatoes. Cook with the onion for about 3 minutes, stirring as needed.

6. Add the ground beef substitute, garlic, 1 teaspoon salt, 1 teaspoon pepper, sage, and Worcestershire sauce. Cook until browned.

7. Stir in the frozen vegetables. Cook until tender. Remove from the heat. Set aside. Remember, this will cook in the oven, so do not overcook on the stove top.

8. In an 8″ skillet, melt the butter on medium heat. Add the flour and stir vigorously.

9. When the flour and butter become a deep beige color, reduce the heat to low and slowly add the milk or half-and-half, vegetable stock, and remaining salt and pepper.

10. Whisk the mixture until it's thick and bubbly and coats the back of a spoon.

11. Pour into the meat and vegetable mixture. Season with salt and pepper.

12. Spoon into the ramekins until they are about ¾ full.

13. Cut the remaining piecrust into three pieces. Place a piece over each pot pie, using a fork to seal the edges.

14. In a 1.5-quart mixing bowl, mix the egg with the water. Brush the egg wash on the crust of each ramekin.

15. Use a knife to cut a small slit in the top of the pastry.

16. Place the ramekins on a baking sheet. Bake for 30–35 minutes.

17. The tops should be golden brown when finished. Cool for 5 minutes before serving.

Sloppy Joes

SERVES 4–6

This iconic American meal is a go-to dinner option for many households. My meat-free version of this classic comfort food is delicious and easy to prepare: It's a one-skillet dish! I can have it on the table in under 30 minutes (with minimal cleanup afterward), and I can feel good knowing it's healthy and homemade. It's a win-win recipe for every home chef. Serve with a side salad or veggies.

1 tablespoon olive oil

1 medium yellow onion, diced

12 ounces ground beef substitute

2 garlic cloves, minced

2 tablespoons tomato paste

1 teaspoon chili powder

1 teaspoon ground mustard

½ teaspoon salt

1 14.5-ounce can diced tomatoes with green chilies

1 tablespoon Worcestershire sauce

1½ cups tomato sauce

1 tablespoon honey

2 tablespoons unsalted butter

4–6 hamburger buns or rolls

1. In a 10″ skillet, heat the olive oil on medium heat.

2. Add the onion. Cook until translucent.

3. Add the ground beef substitute, garlic, tomato paste, chili powder, ground mustard, and salt. Cook on medium heat until browned.

4. Add the tomatoes, Worcestershire sauce, tomato sauce, honey, and butter to the ground beef substitute mixture. Stir to combine. Continue cooking for about 5 minutes, or until hot and bubbly. Season with salt and pepper.

5. Spoon the Sloppy Joe mixture onto the buns and serve immediately.

Note: For a spicy Sloppy Joe, add 1 teaspoon of red pepper flakes with the tomato sauce and honey.

Beef and Broccoli Noodles

SERVES 4–6

Beef and Broccoli Noodles is one of my go-to weeknight meals. It takes about 20–25 minutes to prepare and satisfies all the flavor cravings. It's fragrant, savory, and spicy all at once. You can prepare this dish with rice noodles like I do, or you can swap in buckwheat or ramen noodles. The sauce for this recipe also makes a fantastic marinade or glaze, so make a little extra to store in the fridge.

SAUCE

½ cup tamari sauce (or soy sauce)

½ cup brown sugar

5 tablespoons hoisin sauce

1 teaspoon roasted red chili paste

3 garlic cloves, minced

1 teaspoon ground ginger

BEEF AND BROCCOLI NOODLES

2–3 ounces rice noodles

2 cups broccoli florets or 1 medium head of broccoli

1 tablespoon olive oil

2 teaspoons sesame oil

6 ounces ground beef substitute

1 tablespoon sesame seeds for garnish

½ cup chopped green onions for garnish

TO MAKE THE SAUCE

In a 5-quart mixing bowl, combine the tamari, brown sugar, hoisin, chili paste, garlic, and ground ginger. Set aside.

TO MAKE THE NOODLES

1. Place the rice noodles in an 8-quart heat-resistant bowl. Place the broccoli on top of the noodles.

2. Boil 8 cups of water and pour to cover the broccoli and noodles. Let the mixture sit for 1–2 minutes. Remove the broccoli with tongs. Set aside.

3. Drain the rice noodles and toss with olive oil. Set aside.

4. In a 10″ skillet, warm the sesame oil on medium heat.

5. Add the ground beef substitute. Cook until browned.

6. Add ½ of the sauce and cook on medium until combined.

7. Add the broccoli and continue to cook for about 2 minutes.

8. Turn into a large mixing bowl and toss with the remaining sauce and noodles.

9. Place on individual plates or serve family style. Garnish with sesame seeds and green onions. Serve immediately.

Beef and Cheese Quesadillas

SERVES 4

There are times when I crave comfort food with all the warm spicy flavors of a complex Latin meal, but I don't have the time to prepare one. That's why I love this recipe. It's super simple, completely vegetarian, and satisfies all the flavor cravings without all the fuss. It's family friendly and time friendly. I make it for 1 or 20, and it always gets rave reviews. You can also make it your own by adding or substituting your favorite veggies. I used fire roasted canned diced tomatoes in this one. Get creative with this recipe and feel good about cooking a healthy, quick dinner for yourself and the ones you love.

2 tablespoons olive oil

12 ounces ground beef substitute

½ teaspoon salt

½ teaspoon pepper

¼ cup chipotle peppers in adobo sauce, pureed

½ cup water

1 cup corn (off the cob or frozen corn thawed)

1 cup diced tomatoes

¼ cup black beans, drained and rinsed

½ cup sliced red, yellow, and green sweet peppers, divided

1 tablespoon unsalted butter

8 flour tortillas

2 cups shredded cheddar cheese

Sour cream, additional peppers, and salsa (optional) for topping

Spicy ranch (optional) for dipping

1. In a 10″ skillet, heat the olive oil on medium heat.

2. Add the ground beef substitute, salt, and pepper. Cook until browned, 2–3 minutes.

3. Add the chipotle peppers and water.

4. Cook until bubbly, about 2 minutes.

5. Add the corn, tomatoes, black beans, and ½ of the sweet peppers.

6. Cook on medium heat until mixture is hot and bubbly, 2–3 minutes.

7. Remove from the heat. Set aside.

8. In a 10″skillet, melt 1 tablespoon of butter on medium heat. Don't let the butter burn.

9. Place 2 tortillas in the skillet to brown in the butter. Flip each tortilla and brown on the other side.

10. Add the mixture to one of the tortillas, top with ¼ of the cheese, cover with the second tortilla, and press with a spatula.

11. Cook until cheese melts.

12. Continue the process until all 4 quesadillas are cooked.

13. Cut into quarters and serve family style.

14. Top with sour cream, additional peppers, salsa, and/or a side of spicy ranch for dipping.

Beefy Baked Sweet Potatoes

SERVES 4

I've added a ground beef substitute to this down-home recipe to create a hearty vegetarian meal packed with flavor and all the nutrients needed to make it through a busy day. Some would say I'm obsessed with Chinese five-spice powder. Its sweet and fragrant flavor profile is hypnotic, offering hints of licorice from the star anise and the fennel, which align well with the cinnamon. If you can't find Chinese five-spice powder, or are not fond of these flavors, you can substitute with chili powder or your favorite hamburger seasoning.

4 medium sweet potatoes

1½ teaspoons salt, divided

2 cups broccoli florets

1 tablespoon olive oil

6–8 ounces ground beef substitute

2 garlic cloves, minced

1 teaspoon onion powder

½ teaspoon pepper

1 teaspoon Chinese five-spice powder

3 tablespoons unsalted butter

1 medium shallot, diced

1 cup shredded cheddar cheese

1 cup cottage cheese (optional)

1. Preheat oven to 350 degrees F.

2. Rinse sweet potatoes and wrap in aluminum foil. Pierce each sweet potato with a knife. Place on a baking sheet. Bake in the center of your oven for 50–55 minutes.

3. In a 5-quart saucepan or stockpot, bring salted water (add about 1 teaspoon of salt) to a boil.

4. Add the broccoli florets to the boiling water to blanch, 30–60 seconds. They will become bright green.

5. Remove the broccoli from the water and place in an ice bath for 2–3 minutes. Drain and set aside.

6. In an 8″ skillet, heat the olive oil on medium heat.

7. Add ground beef substitute, garlic, onion powder, remaining ½ teaspoon of salt, pepper, and Chinese five-spice powder to the skillet. Cook until browned.

8. Remove to a heat-resistant bowl. Set aside

9. In the same skillet, melt the butter. Add the shallot and cook on medium heat until fragrant and translucent.

10. Add the broccoli to the skillet and stir until it is covered in the butter and shallots. Season with salt.

11. Remove the sweet potatoes when finished (they should be easily pierced with a knife or fork). Remove the foil and let them cool.

12. Slice each down the middle but not all the way through. Make a cavity in each sweet potato and fill it with the ground beef substitute and broccoli mixtures in layers. Top with the cheddar.

13. Place on the baking sheet and return to the oven for 5–7 minutes, just long enough to melt the cheese.

14. Remove from the oven to cool. Top with cottage cheese and a sprinkle of Chinese five-spice powder for garnish.

Note: You can substitute sour cream or ricotta cheese for the cottage cheese.

Bruschetta Pastina with Beef

SERVES 4

I'm fortunate to have married into a huge Italian family that is passionate about their food. I've listened and learned through the years and have come to understand that Italian food shouldn't be fussy. It's about using what you have, making it with love, and bringing your family together for a shared meal. It's this little nugget of insight that helped me create *Bruschetta Pastina with Beef.* Now that ground beef substitutes are readily available, I can make this dish for everyone in my household. If you're not familiar with pastina, it's a tiny pasta (its name means "tiny dough"). It's considered a comfort food in Italy and is served with cheese and eggs. This particular recipe encapsulates everything I love about Italian food—freshness, simplicity, comfort, and flavor.

2 cups water

1 cup pastina

½ cup cream or half-and-half, room temperature

¼ cup Fontina cheese (or white cheddar or Parmesan)

1 teaspoon salt, divided

3 tablespoons olive oil, divided

12 ounces ground beef substitute

½ teaspoon pepper

½ teaspoon dried basil (or 1 teaspoon chopped fresh basil)

½ teaspoon dried parsley (or 1 teaspoon chopped fresh parsley)

4 garlic cloves, chopped

12–16 ounces cherry tomatoes, halved

½ teaspoon red pepper flakes

1 cup spinach

Shredded mozzarella cheese or Parmesan cheese for topping

1. In an 8-quart stockpot, bring the water to a boil. Add the pastina.

2. Lower the heat to medium and add the cream. Let this mixture simmer on medium low for about 5 minutes, or until pasta mixture is smooth. Remove from the heat and add the Fontina and ½ teaspoon of salt. Cover and set aside.

3. In a 10″ skillet, heat 2 tablespoons of the olive oil on medium heat.

4. Add ground beef substitute, the remaining ½ teaspoon of salt, pepper, basil, and parsley. Combine and cook until browned.

5. Add the garlic and the tomatoes, and heat until the tomatoes blister and the garlic is soft, but not browned.

6. Stir in the red pepper flakes. Remove from the heat.

7. In a 6″ skillet, heat the remaining olive oil on medium heat.

8. Add the spinach and a pinch of salt. Toss to coat and warm the spinach. Do not wilt the greens: They should just be warmed and coated.

9. Spoon the cheesy pastina into pasta bowls and place warmed greens on the pastina. Layer the bruschetta beef mixture on top.

10. Top with the shredded mozzarella cheese or Parmesan.

Note: This recipe is all about the flavor, so if your garlic cloves are small, feel free to add 1 or 2 more. The spinach can be omitted from this recipe or replaced with shaved brussels sprouts or arugula.

Cheeseburger Soup

SERVES 4–6

This is a meat-free version of a premium comfort food that will stand up to the test of your pickiest eater. It's also an easy, one-pot meal that you can serve family style and have each person customize with garnishes like pickles, relish, shredded cheddar, chopped green onions, pickled jalapeño peppers, and crispy fried onions. Serve with a side of crusty sourdough bread or Hawaiian rolls.

2 tablespoons olive oil

1 red onion, diced

2 garlic cloves, minced

12 ounces ground beef substitute

1 teaspoon onion powder

1 medium russet potato, cut into small cubes

1 16-ounce can diced tomatoes

2 ½ cups vegetable stock

1 cup heavy cream

½ teaspoon salt

½ teaspoon pepper

½ teaspoon red pepper flakes (optional)

2 cups shredded cheddar cheese (or pepper jack for more spice)

1. In an 8-quart saucepan or stockpot, heat the olive oil. Add the onion. Cook for 2 minutes.

2. Add the garlic and cook just to warm, about 1 minute (do not burn the garlic). Add the ground beef substitute and onion powder. Cook until browned.

3. Add the potatoes and tomatoes to the mixture. Continue to cook.

4. Add the vegetable stock and heavy cream, stirring to combine.

5. Add the salt and pepper, and red pepper flakes for a spicier soup.

6. Cover and simmer for about 10 minutes.

7. Add the cheese and stir until melted.

8. Season with salt.

Ground Beef Stroganoff

SERVES 3–6

I completely adore any dish that includes sour cream. It's a staple ingredient for me because it makes an easy sauce for just about anything, and this *Ground Beef Stroganoff* is no exception. I serve this creamy dish with a salad to lighten up a very rich meal. The key to this dish is layering the flavors, from the sautéed onions to the coarse ground pepper. (Keep in mind that course ground pepper is always best used when half is added at the beginning of cooking the dish and the rest is added at the end.) Customize this dish so that the flavors work just right for you.

1 8-ounce package egg noodles

2 tablespoons unsalted butter, divided

1 tablespoon olive oil

1 medium yellow onion, diced

1 teaspoon coarse ground pepper

12 ounces ground beef substitute

2 garlic cloves, minced

1 tablespoon Worcestershire sauce

1 teaspoon salt

1 cup sliced cremini mushrooms (or baby bellos)

1 cup vegetable stock

1 cup sour cream

1–2 tablespoons chopped parsley for garnish

1. In a 6-quart saucepan or stockpot, heat water to boiling and add the egg noodles. Cook until tender, drain (do not rinse), turn into a large mixing bowl or pasta bowl, and add 1 tablespoon of the butter to coat the noodles and keep them from sticking together.

2. In a 10″ skillet, heat the olive oil on medium heat.

3. Add the onion and ½ teaspoon of the pepper, and the remaining butter. Cook until the onion is barely translucent.

4. Add the ground beef substitute, garlic, Worcestershire sauce, and salt. Cook until browned, about 3 minutes. The ground beef substitute will cook faster than regular ground beef, so browning time will be shorter.

5. When the ground beef substitute mixture is browned, add the mushrooms and vegetable stock, and cook for about 3 minutes or until nice and bubbly.

6. Stir in the sour cream until it's fully incorporated.

7. Add the remaining ½ teaspoon of pepper and salt to taste.

8. Add the noodles and cook a few minutes until the entire mixture is steamy and bubbly.

9. Serve immediately in pasta bowls and garnish with chopped parsley.

Note: If you don't have sour cream, you can always substitute with cream cheese—however, you will need to increase the vegetable stock to 1½ cups.

Harissa Street Tacos with Pickled Veggies

SERVES 4

During one "meatless Monday" meal prep at home, I realized I had everything for meatless tacos except the seasoning, so I created this delicious version of beef tacos with a ground beef substitute and harissa seasoning. Harissa is spicy and tangy and pairs perfectly with these tacos. It's available in most grocery stores and is often used in traditional meat dishes to kick up the flavors of stews and slow-cooked chicken recipes. Everyone loved these tacos so much, they're now a staple on my dinner menu.

PICKLED VEGGIES

1¼ cups mango nectar

1 cup rice vinegar

2 tablespoons light agave

1½ cups julienned carrots

1½ cups sliced red onion

1½ cups purple cabbage

TACOS

12 ounces ground beef substitute

1 teaspoon garlic powder

1 teaspoon onion powder

1 teaspoon salt

1 teaspoon harissa powder or
taco seasoning

1 tablespoon olive oil

½ cup tomato sauce

2 tablespoons water

1 tablespoon butter

Flour or white corn tortillas

Feta, cotija, or cheddar cheese
for garnish

TO MAKE THE PICKLED VEGGIES

1. Prepare the pickled veggies first. This can also be done a day or two ahead and stored in the refrigerator.

2. In a 5-quart saucepan, add the mango nectar, vinegar, and agave. Warm on low heat until it begins to simmer. Remove from the heat. Set aside.

3. Place the veggies in three separate non-reactive metal or heat-tolerant ceramic dishes. Don't pickle these veggies together because the purple color of the onions and the cabbage will stain the orange carrots brown.

4. Add equal amounts of the warm pickling liquid to all three veggie bowls. Set aside to cool. Once cool, store in any type of food containers. I use glass mason jars or glass flip top jars. They go from the refrigerator to the table and look great!

TO MAKE THE TACOS

1. In a 5-quart mixing bowl, add the ground beef substitute, garlic powder, onion powder, salt, and harissa or taco seasoning. Mix well.

2. In an 8" skillet, heat the olive oil on medium heat.

3. Add the beef substitute mixture to the skillet. Cook until browned.

4. Add the tomato sauce, water, and butter, stirring until combined.

5. Cook until the mixture just begins to bubble.

6. Wrap the tortillas in a paper towel and warm them in a microwave. Or place tortillas one at a time in a dry skillet to warm.

7. Place the taco "meat" on the individual tortillas and serve with the pickled veggies and cheese for garnish.

Salisbury Steak with Parmesan and Chive Mashers

SERVES 4–6

Salisbury steak and mashed potatoes is one of the home-cooked meals I remember my grandmother making for me when I was young. Just barely tall enough to peek over the stove, I watched her magically transform these wonderful little meat patties into something so delicious. Today, I still get all that feeling when I make this dish. It's lovely to know that I'm re-creating a home-cooked meal that's rich in memories, and that because of the advances in meat substitutes, my whole family can enjoy it.

SALISBURY STEAK

12 ounces ground beef substitute

½ cup seasoned bread crumbs

1 teaspoon onion powder

1 teaspoon garlic powder

1 teaspoon Worcestershire sauce

½ teaspoon salt

½ teaspoon pepper

1 tablespoon olive oil

GRAVY

1 tablespoon olive oil

1 cup diced onions

2 tablespoons unsalted butter

2 tablespoons flour

1½ cups vegetable stock, room temperature

½ cup white wine, room temperature

1½ cups sliced mushrooms

3 dashes Worcestershire sauce

TO MAKE THE SALISBURY STEAK

1. In a 5-quart mixing bowl, add the ground beef substitute, bread crumbs, onion powder, garlic powder, Worcestershire sauce, salt, and pepper. Use your hands to combine.

2. Use your hands to form 4–6 patties. Set aside.

3. In a 10″ skillet, warm the olive oil on medium heat. Place the patties in the skillet and cook each side for 1–2 minutes, turning gently, until done. Remove from heat (which can cause them to crumble) and cover with foil.

TO MAKE THE GRAVY

1. In the same skillet heat the olive oil on medium heat. Add the onions and cook until slightly translucent.

2. Add the butter and flour, stirring well.

3. When the butter, flour, and onion mixture turns a deep beige, reduce the heat to low and slowly add the vegetable stock and wine, stirring with a whisk to combine.

4. Whisk the mixture until it's thick and bubbly and coats the back of a spoon. Add the mushrooms, Worcestershire sauce, salt, and pepper.

5. Continue to stir the gravy until hot and bubbly. Add the butter, stirring to blend it into the sauce.

1½ teaspoons salt

¼ teaspoon pepper

1 tablespoon butter

PARMESAN AND CHIVE MASHERS

3–4 medium russet potatoes, peeled and cut into ½″ pieces

¼ cup chopped fresh chives (or 2 tablespoons dried chives)

3 tablespoons shredded Parmesan cheese

½ cup half-and-half or heavy cream

2 tablespoons unsalted butter

6. Remove the gravy off the heat. Add the meat patties, gently covering them with the sauce.

7. Serve homestyle by placing steaks and gravy on a large serving platter.

TO MAKE THE MASHERS

1. In a 6-quart saucepan or stockpot, add the potatoes to salted water and heat on medium high heat. Cook until potatoes are tender.

2. Drain the potatoes and place in an 8-quart mixing bowl.

3. Add the chives, Parmesan, half-and-half, butter, salt, and pepper.

4. Use a potato masher or a large wooden spoon to combine. The mashers will be chunky.

5. Season with salt and pepper.

Tuxedo Pasta Bake

SERVES 6

If fettuccini Alfredo had a cousin, this would be it. The *Tuxedo Pasta Bake* is a family-style pasta dish with all the warm and fuzzy feels of fettuccini Alfredo but without the fuss. Start with a hearty plant-based meat component, add in some Boursin cheese, some cream, and some mushrooms, and you've got the best comfort food flavors all in one casserole dish. This meal is easy to prepare and fun to serve at a family or dinner party. Serve with a Caesar salad, a bottle of sauvignon blanc, and enjoy!

---

12 ounces bowtie (farfalle) pasta

1 tablespoon olive oil

1 medium shallot, sliced into thin pieces

12 ounces ground beef substitute

½ teaspoon salt

1 garlic clove, minced

2½ ounces Boursin basil and chive cheese

4 tablespoons unsalted butter

1½ cups heavy cream

½ cup vegetable stock

1 cup sliced cremini or baby bello mushrooms

¼ cup sliced black olives

1½ cups shredded mozzarella cheese

1. Preheat oven to 350 degrees F.

2. Cook pasta in salted water until al dente. Drain and rinse when cooked.

3. In a 10″ skillet, heat the olive oil on medium heat.

4. Add shallot and cook until caramelized.

5. Add the ground beef substitute, salt, and garlic. Cook until browned.

6. Add the Boursin. Mix until melted.

7. Add the butter, cream, and vegetable stock to the ground beef substitute and Boursin mixture. Cook for 2–4 minutes.

8. Add mushrooms and cook for 2 minutes.

9. Add the pasta and olives (save a few for the garnish) to the mixture. Remove from the heat and pour into a 2-quart or 13″ x 9″ baking dish.

10. Top with the mozzarella and a line of black olives down the middle. (It'll look like a tuxedo.)

11. Bake for 15–20 minutes until the cheese melts and lightly browns.

12. Remove from the oven and let it rest for 5 minutes before serving.

Note: This recipe has a very rich sauce, so I recommend serving it with a light side salad and pairing with a dry white wine to complement the flavors.

Creamy Mac and Cheese with Spicy Beef and Sautéed Onions

SERVES 4–6

Mac and cheese shouldn't have to be made from a box or a packet of powdered cheese. This recipe is so easy, you'll be ready to ditch the boxed version forever. The best part is getting creative with toppings. I typically top this recipe with sautéed onions. But you can try mushrooms, broccoli, and additional cheeses.

16 ounces macaroni pasta

2 tablespoons olive oil, divided

1 onion, sliced

¼ cup vegetable stock

12 ounces ground beef substitute

2 garlic cloves, minced

¼ teaspoon onion powder

½ teaspoon red pepper flakes (optional)

9 tablespoons unsalted butter, divided

2 cups heavy cream

2 cups shredded cheddar cheese

2½ ounces Boursin black pepper cheese

1. Cook the macaroni according to the package directions. Drain and set aside.

2. In an 8" skillet, heat 1 tablespoon of the olive oil on medium heat. Add the onion and cook on medium heat until translucent.

3. Reduce the heat to low and add the vegetable stock. Let the stock simmer for 20 minutes.

4. In an 8" skillet, heat the remaining olive oil on medium heat.

5. Add the ground beef substitute, garlic, onion powder, and red pepper flakes. Cook until browned. Set aside.

6. In a 5-quart saucepan, heat 8 tablespoons of the butter and heavy cream on low heat and bring to a low simmer. Do not boil.

7. Add the cheddar and Boursin to the saucepan on low heat to melt. Stir to combine.

8. Add the pasta to the cream and cheese mixture. Remove from the heat. Stir to coat the noodles.

9. Gently fold the ground beef substitute mixture into the noodles and cheese.

10. Spoon into individual pasta bowls.

11. Remove the onions from the heat and add the remaining 1 tablespoon of butter. Top each mac and cheese serving with the cooked onions and enjoy.

Flatbread Pizza

SERVES 4

I'm a fan of about any kind of greens, and arugula is a favorite. Its deep green color and peppery flavor add depth (and nutrients!) to many recipes, including this one. If you're trying to add greens to your or your family's diet, why not on pizza? To make this an even bigger win, this *Flatbread Pizza* is entirely vegetarian when you use ground beef substitute. I've also kicked up the heat a bit with pickled jalapeño peppers, though you can leave them out if you prefer your pizza less spicy. I included balsamic glaze for topping, but you might also add ranch dressing, sliced red onion, black olives, mushrooms, or green peppers. Experiment and enjoy!

4 individual flatbreads

2 tablespoons olive oil, divided

12 ounces ground beef substitute

½ teaspoon salt

½ teaspoon pepper

½ teaspoon dried oregano

2 garlic cloves, minced

1 14-ounce jar pizza sauce

16 ounces shredded mozzarella, divided

1 large tomato, thinly sliced

Pickled jalapeño peppers (optional)

4 ounces arugula or spinach

Balsamic glaze (optional)

1. Preheat oven to 425 degrees F.

2. Brush the flatbreads with ½ of the olive oil and place on a baking sheet or pizza peel.

3. Place the flatbreads in the oven for 5–7 minutes or until lightly toasted.

4. In a 10" skillet, heat the remaining olive oil on medium heat. Add the ground beef substitute, salt, pepper, oregano, and garlic. Cook on medium heat until browned.

5. Spread the pizza sauce 1 tablespoon at a time on the flatbreads.

6. Sprinkle half of the mozzarella evenly over the flatbreads. Layer on the ground beef substitute mixture, tomatoes, and jalapeños.

7. Return to the oven for 7–10 minutes, or until the tops are golden brown and the cheese has melted.

8. Remove from the oven and cool for 3–5 minutes.

9. Place a handful of arugula in the center of each flatbread pizza and sprinkle with the remaining mozzarella.

10. Drizzle each with balsamic glaze.

Meatloaf with Onion Gravy

SERVES 4–6

Meatloaf is one of those all-American meals my mom would make to stretch the weekly food budget. I am forever experimenting with new meatloaf recipes to bring this vintage meal into the future, and this plant-based version is a winner worth sharing. It satisfies the need for comfort food and a healthy vegetarian meal without sacrificing flavor. I created a sweet onion gravy to take that flavor to the limit. Hint: Make extra gravy to use as a topping for sautéed vegetables, eggs, or savory bread.

MEATLOAF

1 15-ounce can chickpeas, drained and rinsed

1 tablespoon milk

½ cup seasoned bread crumbs

12 ounces ground beef substitute

1 small sweet onion, diced

1 cup tomato sauce

1 tablespoon Worcestershire sauce

1 large egg

1 teaspoon salt

½ teaspoon pepper

1 teaspoon garlic powder

½ cup shredded cheddar cheese

ONION GRAVY

2 tablespoons butter

2 sweet onions, thinly sliced

½ cup white wine

1½ tablespoons honey

2 tablespoons vegetable stock

TO MAKE THE MEATLOAF

1. Preheat oven to 350 degrees F.

2. Line a loaf pan with parchment paper.

3. Mash the chickpeas with a potato masher or blend them in a food processor until smooth.

4. Add the milk to the bread crumbs and let them soak for a minute.

5. Add the chickpeas, soaked bread crumbs, ground beef substitute, onion, tomato sauce, Worcestershire sauce, egg, salt, pepper, garlic powder, and cheddar to an 8-quart mixing bowl. Use your hands to mix thoroughly.

6. Place the mixture in the loaf pan. Bake covered for 30 minutes. Uncover and bake for an additional 15–20 minutes.

7. Remove the meatloaf from the oven and let it sit for 3–4 minutes.

8. Serve covered with the gravy.

TO MAKE THE GRAVY

1. In a 6-quart sauté pan, melt the butter on medium heat. Add the onions and cook until translucent.

2. Add white wine, honey, vegetable stock, and a sprinkle of salt and pepper.

3. Let the mixture simmer on low heat for about 20 minutes. Remove from the heat when the onions are lightly browned. Season with salt and pepper.

4. Serve on top of the meatloaf.

Note: The sweet *Onion Gravy* is a tasty complement to the meatloaf, but barbeque sauce and honey mustard sauce are also worthy alternatives.

Spaghetti Squash with Beef and Burrata

SERVES 4

Spaghetti squash is a great dinner vegetable, especially when I'm attempting to decrease the number of times I cook and serve pasta at home. A few years ago, I came up with this alternative recipe for pasta night, and everyone loved it. Since then, I've discovered I can make it for my meat eaters *and* my vegetarians by preparing it with a ground beef substitute. It tastes equally delicious.

2 medium spaghetti squash

2 tablespoons olive oil, divided

12 ounces ground beef substitute

2 garlic cloves, minced

1¼ cup jarred pasta sauce or
Sunday Sauce (see page 76)

1 tablespoon butter

8 ounces burrata (2 pieces)

½ teaspoon coarse ground pepper
for garnish

Shredded Parmesan cheese for garnish

Chopped basil for garnish

Olive oil for garnish

1. Preheat oven to 425 degrees F.

2. Cut the spaghetti squash in half lengthwise and clean out the seeds.

3. Rub the cut side with olive oil and season with salt and pepper.

4. Place the spaghetti squash, flesh-side down, on a parchment-lined baking sheet.

5. Bake the squash for 20 minutes.

6. In a 10″ skillet, warm the remaining olive oil on medium heat. Add the ground beef substitute and garlic. Cook until browned.

7. Add the *Sunday Sauce* (or jarred sauce) and cook until warm and simmering.

8. Remove the spaghetti squash from the oven. Set aside to cool.

9. When cooled, use a fork to scrape the inside of the squash, creating spaghetti-like strands. Save the squash skins.

10. Place squash in a 3-quart bowl. Add the butter and ¼ cup of *Sunday Sauce*. Toss to coat.

11. Cut each burrata piece in half to make 4 pieces.

12. Spoon the squash mixture into the squash skins, top with the ground beef substitute mixture and a piece of burrata.

13. Place in the oven for 5 minutes to lightly melt the cheese and warm the squash.

14. Garnish with pepper, Parmesan, basil, a drizzle of olive oil, and a little more *Sunday Sauce*.

Spaghetti Casserole

SERVES 4–6

I was introduced to *Spaghetti Casserole* when I lived in Texas. I showed up to a friend's house for dinner just in time to see her mom remove the most massive casserole dish I'd ever seen from her oven and declare in a thick accent that the spaghetti casserole was ready. I had never heard of it before that day, but I remember taking the first bite and thinking to myself, *Where have you been all of my life?* This recipe is Italian food Texas-style, with a bold, rich flavor and layers of cheesy goodness.

3 tablespoons butter, divided

16 ounces spaghetti pasta

2 large eggs

2 cups ricotta cheese

1 cup sour cream

¼ cup shredded Parmesan cheese

2 tablespoons olive oil

1 yellow or white onion, diced

2 garlic cloves, diced

1 teaspoon Italian seasoning

12 ounces ground beef substitute

½ teaspoon salt

½ teaspoon pepper

24 ounces jarred pasta sauce
or *Sunday Sauce* (see page 76)

1½ cups shredded cheddar cheese

1½ cups shredded mozzarella cheese

1. Preheat oven to 375 degrees F.

2. Grease a 9″ x 13″ casserole dish with 1 tablespoon of the butter.

3. Cook the spaghetti according to package directions. Drain well and return to the stockpot.

4. Add the eggs, ricotta cheese, sour cream, and Parmesan to the spaghetti and mix well. Set aside.

5. In an 8″ skillet, heat the olive oil on medium heat. Add the onion, garlic, Italian seasoning, and remaining butter.

6. Cook the onion until translucent, 1–2 minutes. Add the ground beef substitute, salt, and pepper. Cook until browned.

7. Add 2 cups of the pasta sauce to the mixture. Stir to combine. Set aside.

8. Place ½ of the spaghetti mixture in the baking dish.

9. Place ½ of the ground beef substitute mixture on the spaghetti.

10. Add a final layer of spaghetti and top with a layer of the ground beef substitute mixture.

11. Cover with the remaining pasta sauce.

12. Sprinkle the cheddar and mozzarella over the top, and place in the oven.

13. Cook for 30–35 minutes, or until the cheese is bubbly and golden brown.

14. Cool for 5 minutes and cut into squares.

Note: I've tried both spaghetti and angel hair pasta in this recipe. The spaghetti works best with the thick sauce and cheese, but angel hair or vermicelli can be used as a substitute.

Stuffed Pepper Soup

SERVES 4–6

Stuffed peppers is a quintessential dinner for many families. Where I grew up, it was typically chili rellenos that made its way to the table, but on occasion, it was stuffed peppers. Today, I make a beef substitute version of stuffed peppers that features the dish's main attraction, the bell peppers. I also add a little hometown flavor with Tajín seasoning. If I'm feeling especially spicy, I add a chopped jalapeño pepper. Top this with a little creamy pepper jack and enjoy!

---

4 tablespoons olive oil, divided

2 bell peppers, diced

1 medium yellow onion, diced

4 cups vegetable stock

2 teaspoons Tajín seasoning

½ cup quick-cooking rice

12 ounces ground beef substitute

2 garlic cloves, minced

½ teaspoon salt

½ teaspoon pepper

1 green onion, chopped, for garnish

¼ cup shredded pepper jack cheese for garnish (optional)

1. In a 5- or 8-quart stockpot, heat 2 tablespoons of the olive oil on medium heat.

2. Add the peppers and onion. Cook until the onion is translucent.

3. Add vegetable stock, Tajín seasoning, and rice. Cook on medium heat and bring to a simmer. Turn to low and simmer covered for 15 minutes.

4. In an 8″ skillet, heat the remaining olive oil on medium heat.

5. Add the ground beef substitute, garlic, salt, and pepper. Cook until browned.

6. When the pepper and rice mixture has finished simmering, add the ground beef substitute mixture, and simmer for 10 minutes.

7. Serve in soup bowls or mugs. Top with green onion or pepper jack cheese.

Note: If you'd like to make this a spicier dish, add a diced jalapeño along with the peppers and onion in step two.

Beef Orecchiette with Lemon Cream Sauce

SERVES 4–6

I discovered orecchiette pasta years ago at one of my favorite Italian restaurants in New York City. It was cooked perfectly, and every piece was covered in a delectable cream sauce. Orecchiette, or "little ears" (named for its ear-like shape), originated in Puglia, a southern region of Italy, and has become one of my favorite pastas. Most of the time you will see orecchiette served with broccoli. In this dish I combine my love of *Lemon Cream Sauce* and beef to create a quick and easy pasta meal the entire family will enjoy. It's Italian comfort food that makes you feel like you're at Nonna's house.

4 tablespoons olive oil, divided

12 ounces ground beef substitute

3 garlic cloves, minced

½ teaspoon coarse ground pepper

1 onion, diced

1 cup vegetable stock, room temperature

1 tablespoon lemon juice

1 teaspoon lemon zest

2 cups heavy cream, room temperature

1½ cups orecchiette pasta

1 cup shredded Parmesan cheese

3 tablespoons butter

1. In an 8″ skillet, warm 2 tablespoons of the olive oil on medium heat.

2. Add the ground beef substitute and garlic. Cook on medium heat until browned. Set aside.

3. In a 10″ skillet, add remaining olive oil, pepper, and onion. Cook on medium heat until the onion is translucent.

4. Add vegetable stock, lemon juice, lemon zest, and cream. Stir to combine.

5. Add the orecchiette. Simmer on low heat until the pasta is al dente.

6. When the orecchiette is ready, remove from the heat. Add ½ cup of the Parmesan, butter, and the ground beef substitute. Stir to combine.

7. Serve immediately in pasta bowls and garnish with the remaining Parmesan.

Note: Cooking the pasta in the vegetable stock and cream allows for a luxurious sauce, but you can add moisture by pouring in additional vegetable stock while simmering.

Pasta Bolognese

SERVES 4–6

Bolognese is a hearty sauce traditionally served on homemade tagliatelle pasta. If I can't find tagliatelle, I purchase pappardelle or thick spaghetti. I love to make homemade pasta for this sauce. It's a fun family-night event at our house, but it makes a big mess in the kitchen and is time consuming. If you're more interested in getting dinner on the table, this is the perfect option and takes about 30 minutes.

16 ounces pasta (tagliatelle, pappardelle, or thick spaghetti)

2 tablespoons unsalted butter

¼ cup olive oil

1 medium onion, diced

1 carrot, peeled and coarsely chopped

1 celery stalk, diced

3 garlic cloves, coarsely chopped

1 teaspoon salt

1 teaspoon coarse ground pepper

2 tablespoons basil, chopped (or 1½ teaspoons dried basil)

12 ounces ground beef substitute

1 28-ounce can diced or crushed tomatoes

¼ cup red wine

½ cup shredded Parmesan cheese

1. Cook the pasta according to the package directions. Drain and place in a 5-quart mixing bowl. Add the butter. Toss to coat.

2. In a 10″ skillet, warm the olive oil on medium high heat.

3. Add the onion, carrot, and celery. Cook for 5–6 minutes.

4. Add garlic, salt, pepper, basil, and ground beef substitute.

5. Cook on medium heat until browned and the vegetables are tender.

6. Add tomatoes and red wine.

7. Simmer on low heat for 20 minutes.

8. Remove from the heat. Add ¼ cup of the Parmesan and stir to melt.

9. Serve with pasta and garnish with remaining Parmesan.

Note: You can substitute the red wine with ¼ cup of the pasta water.

Sausage Cassoulet

SERVES 4–6

A cassoulet is a simple French comfort food often associated with white beans and pork sausage, chicken, and sometimes duck. Named for the cooking pot used to prepare the dish, this vegetarian version of cassoulet embraces its meaty counterpart's rich flavors but in about 30 minutes of cooking time. I love how easy this is to put together for dinner. It looks beautiful in a large serving bowl and tastes delicious with a side of fresh French bread.

14 ounces plant-based Italian sausage

3 tablespoons olive oil, plus more for drizzling

1 medium red onion, cut into chunks

3 garlic cloves, minced

½ teaspoon dried rosemary (or 1 teaspoon chopped fresh rosemary)

½ teaspoon dried tarragon (or 1 teaspoon chopped fresh tarragon)

1 bay leaf

1 14.5-ounce can diced tomatoes

1 15.8-ounce can Great Northern white beans or cannellini beans, drained and rinsed

½ teaspoon salt

½ teaspoon pepper

1 cup vegetable stock

¼ cup white wine

Crusty bread (optional)

1. Cook the plant-based Italian sausage according to package directions. Set aside.

2. In a large stockpot heat the olive oil on medium heat. Add the onion and garlic. Cook the onion and garlic but not to translucent.

3. Add the rosemary, tarragon, bay leaf, tomatoes, beans, salt, pepper, vegetable stock, and wine.

4. Bring to a simmer. Reduce to low heat and simmer uncovered for about 10 minutes.

5. Cut the plant-based sausage into bite-size pieces. Add to the stockpot mixture.

6. Cover and simmer on low for another 20 minutes.

7. Remove the bay leaf. Season with salt and pepper.

8. Serve family style with crusty bread.

Note: Before serving, drizzle with olive oil.

Beef Fried Rice

SERVES 4

Beef Fried Rice is an easy, delicious dinner that makes me feel like everything is right in the world. I love all the Asian flavors in fried rice, from the sesame oil to the tamari and the sambal as a side sauce or garnish. I added beef substitute to make this weeknight meal hearty, filling, and satisfying. This dish can be made in one skillet, so cleanup is a breeze.

2 cups cooked white rice

3 tablespoons olive oil, divided

2 large eggs, lightly beaten

2 tablespoons sesame oil, divided

12 ounces ground beef substitute

½ teaspoon salt

½ teaspoon coarse ground pepper

3 garlic cloves, minced

1 carrot, peeled and diced

3 green onions, chopped

1 cup frozen peas

2 tablespoons tamari or soy sauce

Sambal or Sriracha for garnish

1. In a 10″ skillet, heat 1 tablespoon of the olive oil on medium heat. Add the eggs, and cook until scrambled. Set aside.

2. In the same skillet, on medium heat, add 1 tablespoon of the olive oil and 1 tablespoon of the sesame oil, the ground beef substitute, salt, pepper, and garlic. Cook until browned. Set aside with the eggs.

3. Add the remaining olive oil to the same pan on medium heat. Add the carrot and ¾ of the green onions. Cook until the vegetables are tender, 3–4 minutes.

4. Add the remaining sesame oil to the skillet. Add the egg, ground beef substitute, and rice. Add the frozen peas.

5. Drizzle on the tamari or soy sauce. Stir to combine.

6. Garnish with remaining green onion.

7. Serve family style or in individual bowls. Place tamari or soy sauce, sambal, or Sriracha on the table, and season to taste.

Note: Sambal is a delicious chili paste that adds heat and flavor to any rice dish. It can be found in most markets in the international foods section.

Dirty Rice with Remoulade Sauce

SERVES 4

I first learned to make dirty rice when I lived in the Deep South. A good friend of mine grew up eating her mom's version of this dish and passed it on to me. I had never tasted anything quite like it. It was full of flavor and color, so I was instantly hooked. Since then, I've created several versions of my own with whatever was in my refrigerator. And now, with ground beef substitute, it's easy to make an entirely vegetarian option of this beloved Southern comfort food.

RICE

2 teaspoons paprika

2 teaspoons garlic powder

1 teaspoon onion powder

1 teaspoon dried oregano

½ teaspoon dried thyme

½ teaspoon salt

½ teaspoon pepper

½ teaspoon cayenne

2 tablespoons unsalted butter

3 cups cooked white rice

2 tablespoons olive oil

1 onion, diced

2 bell peppers, sliced

12 ounces ground beef substitute

1 teaspoon minced garlic

REMOULADE SAUCE

1 cup mayonnaise

1 teaspoon paprika

1½ teaspoons Cajun seasoning

½ teaspoon onion powder

1 garlic clove, finely minced

1 tablespoon lemon juice

Dash of hot sauce

TO MAKE THE RICE

1. In a 1.5-quart mixing bowl, add paprika, garlic powder, onion powder, oregano, thyme, salt, pepper, and cayenne.

2. In a 3-quart saucepan, heat the butter on low heat. Add the rice and the spice mix. Stir to coat the rice in the spices and butter. Set aside.

3. In a 10″ skillet, heat the olive oil on medium heat. Add the onion and peppers. Cook until the vegetables are tender but still firm. Add the ground beef substitute and garlic. Cook until browned.

4. Add rice to the mixture. Combine and cook until everything is warm and steamy.

5. Serve family style or in individual bowls and garnish with remoulade sauce.

TO MAKE THE REMOULADE SAUCE

In a 1.5-quart mixing bowl, add the mayonnaise, paprika, Cajun seasoning, onion powder, garlic, lemon juice, hot sauce, and season with salt and pepper. Blend together until smooth.

Beef and Bean Soup

SERVES 4–6

This delicious *Beef and Bean Soup* is similar to the *Sausage Cassoulet*. Its earthy paprika flavor and brothy bean texture make this a popular cold-weather meal, perfect with a helping of fresh bread. It's typically made with sausage or chorizo. This vegetarian version has ground beef substitute and adds additional layers of flavor by incorporating pickled and fresh jalapeño peppers.

2 tablespoons olive oil, divided

1 carrot, peeled and diced

1 large shallot, diced

2 garlic cloves, finely diced

2 15.8-ounce cans Great Northern white beans or cannellini beans, drained and rinsed

1½ cups vegetable stock

1½ teaspoons paprika, divided

½ teaspoon cumin

1 bay leaf

1 teaspoon salt, divided

½ teaspoon coarse ground pepper

12 ounces ground beef substitute

½ teaspoon onion powder

¼ cup chopped pickled jalapeño peppers

1 jalapeño pepper, diced, for garnish

Chopped parsley for garnish

Chopped chives for garnish

1. In a 6-quart stockpot, heat 1 tablespoon of the olive oil on medium heat.

2. Add the carrot, shallot, and garlic. Cook until the vegetables are tender.

3. Add the beans, vegetable stock, 1 teaspoon paprika, cumin, bay leaf, ½ teaspoon salt, and the pepper. Stir until combined. Bring to a simmer. Reduce the heat to low. Simmer for 30 minutes uncovered.

4. In a 1.5-quart mixing bowl, combine the ground beef substitute, remaining paprika, onion powder, and remaining salt. Use your hands to form 1-ounce patties.

5. In a 10″ skillet, heat the remaining 1 tablespoon of olive oil on medium heat. Add the patties. Flip to brown on each side. Set aside to cool..

6. Break the patties in half to create chunky pieces. .Place the cooked pieces into the bean mixture.

7. Simmer for at least 30 minutes. Add the pickled jalapeños and stir gently. Simmer for another 5 minutes.

8. Serve in individual bowls with fresh bread. Garnish with fresh jalapeño, chopped parsley, or chives.

Stuffed Tomatoes with Goat Cheese

SERVES 4

There are hundreds of ways to make stuffed tomatoes, but one of my favorites is with goat cheese. The creamy goat cheese pairs deliciously with the tomatoes and ground beef substitute, making this a satisfying and truly tasty meal. It's quick and easy and allows me to use up leftover rice. I love serving these tomatoes with a side of homemade soup when it's chilly outside, or with a fresh green salad during warmer months.

2 tablespoons olive oil, plus more to drizzle

12 ounces ground beef substitute

1 teaspoon salt, divided

1 teaspoon coarse ground pepper, divided

3 garlic cloves, minced

4 large tomatoes

4 ounces goat cheese, room temperature

1 teaspoon dried chives (or 1½ teaspoons chopped fresh chives)

1 teaspoon dried parsley (or 1½ teaspoons chopped fresh parsley)

1 cup cooked white rice

½ cup shredded mozzarella cheese

1. Preheat oven to 350 degrees F.

2. In a 10″ skillet, heat the olive oil on medium heat. Add the ground beef substitute, ½ teaspoon of salt, ½ teaspoon of pepper, and garlic. Cook until browned. Set aside.

3. Cut off the tops of the tomatoes, discard them, and hollow out the centers. Sprinkle the remaining ½ teaspoon of salt and pepper, and a drizzle of oil on the inside of each. Set aside.

4. In a 3-quart mixing bowl, add goat cheese, chives, and parsley. Mix together well.

5. Add the rice and cooled ground beef substitute to the goat cheese. Stir to combine.

6. Spoon the rice and beef mixture into each tomato. Fill to overflow the tops.

7. Place the tomatoes on a parchment-lined baking sheet. Sprinkle with the mozzarella.

8. Bake for 15–20 minutes. Broil for the last 3 minutes to melt the mozzarella.

Note: If using leftover rice, moisten it with a few tablespoons of vegetable stock or water.

Thai Beef Lettuce Wraps

SERVES 4

I have a deep fondness for Thai food and the flavors and spices used to make it. I could eat these *Thai Beef Lettuce Wraps* for breakfast, lunch, and dinner—that is how much I love them. Something about a lettuce pocket full of tasty morsels of juicy beef makes for a crowd-pleasing flavor adventure. They are entirely vegetarian thanks to the ground beef substitute, but that doesn't mean they don't satisfy. They are dripping with sweet, tangy, spicy flavor.

1 teaspoon minced garlic

½ teaspoon ground ginger

¼ teaspoon chili paste

½ cup hoisin sauce

1 tablespoon rice vinegar

⅓ cup soy sauce

2 tablespoons sesame oil, divided

1 tablespoon olive oil

½ cup chopped green onions

1 carrot, peeled and diced

1 cup diced water chestnuts

12 ounces ground beef substitute

1 head Boston or butter lettuce

1. In a 1.5-quart mixing bowl, add garlic, ginger, chili paste, hoisin sauce, rice vinegar, soy sauce, and 1 tablespoon sesame oil. Set aside.

2. In a 10″ skillet, heat the remaining sesame oil and the olive oil on medium heat. Add the green onions, carrots, and water chestnuts. Cook until vegetables are tender but still firm.

3. Add the ground beef substitute. Cook until browned.

4. Add the sauce to the vegetables and ground beef substitute mixture. Stir to combine.

5. Simmer on low heat until warm and bubbly.

6. Place the lettuce leaves on a platter and the Thai Beef in a large bowl.

7. Serve family style.

Beef and Three Cheese Risotto

SERVES 4

I began making cheesy risotto for my one and only vegetarian in the family. Everyone loved it so much that it was requested almost weekly. With the accessibility of plant-based meats, it was easy to turn our cheesy risotto into a delicious *Beef and Three Cheese Risotto* that makes us feel as though we're eating real ground beef. Enjoy this recipe family-style or in individual bowls with a side of fresh tomatoes and olive oil.

6–8 cups vegetable stock

2 tablespoons olive oil, divided

2 shallots, chopped

2 cups Arborio rice

½ cup dry white wine

12 ounces ground beef substitute

2 garlic cloves, minced

½ teaspoon salt

½ teaspoon coarse ground pepper

½ cup shredded Parmesan cheese, plus more for garnish

½ cup shredded Fontina cheese

½ cup mascarpone cheese

1. In a 10" saucepan, heat the stock to a simmer. Cover and keep warm over low heat.

2. In a 10"–12" stockpot, heat 1 tablespoon of the olive oil on medium heat. Add the shallots. Cook until tender, 4–5 minutes.

3. Add the rice. Stir about 2 minutes. Add the white wine and stir about 1 minute.

4. Stir in 1 cup of the warm broth. Simmer until it is absorbed, stirring frequently. Cook the rice until almost tender, adding the broth ½ cup at a time. Stir often, allowing each addition to be absorbed before adding the next, 25–30 minutes.

5. In an 8" skillet, heat the remaining olive oil. Add the ground beef substitute, garlic, salt, and pepper. Cook until browned.

6. When the risotto is tender, add the cheeses. Add the ground beef substitute mixture. Season with salt and pepper.

7. Transfer to individual bowls and sprinkle with Parmesan. Serve immediately.

Note: You can increase the Parmesan by ½ cup if you don't have, or don't want to use, Fontina. Of course, then it's a two-cheese risotto!

Shepherd's Pie

SERVES 4–6

The ultimate British comfort food, shepherd's pie has made its way across the pond and into our hearts and stomachs. Having experimented with several versions of shepherd's pie, this meatless one is truly my favorite. The ground beef substitute and the potatoes are the stars of this dish. The beauty here is that it can be made completely vegetarian while still tasting like a hearty, "stick to your ribs," savory pie.

3 large russet potatoes, peeled and diced

1 tablespoon salt

2 tablespoons olive oil

1 medium white or yellow onion, diced

1–2 carrots, peeled and diced

1–2 celery stalks, diced

12 ounces ground beef substitute

½ teaspoon allspice

½ teaspoon salt

½ teaspoon pepper

2 tablespoons flour

2 garlic cloves, minced

1–1½ cups vegetable stock

1 tablespoon tomato paste

4 tablespoons butter

¾–1 cup heavy cream

2 cups shredded cheddar cheese

1. Preheat oven to 400 degrees F.

2. Place potatoes and salt in a 6-quart stockpot. Cover potatoes completely with water and boil until tender.

3. In a 10″ skillet, heat the olive oil on medium heat.

4. Add the onion, carrot, and celery. Cook for 2–3 minutes until steamy and tender.

5. Add the ground beef substitute, allspice, salt, pepper, flour, and garlic. Cook until browned.

6. Add the vegetable stock and tomato paste. Stir and cook for about 15 minutes, or until the mixture has thickened. Season with salt and pepper.

7. In a 6-quart mixing bowl, add the potatoes, butter, and cream. Mash together until smooth.

8. Stir 1 cup of the cheese into the potatoes.

9. Spoon the ground beef substitute mixture into a 9″ x 9″ baking dish. Top with the mashed potatoes.

10. Sprinkle the remaining cheese on top of the potatoes. Bake for 25–30 minutes, or until the top is golden brown.

Note: Before filling your baking dish, be sure the ground beef substitute mixture has cooked down and all of the vegetable stock has reduced. You don't want a soggy, watery layer at the bottom of your pie.

Beef and Mushroom Manicotti

SERVES 4–6

This manicotti recipe is a real crowd-pleaser. It's herby and rich and goes from the oven directly to the dinner table without a lot of fuss. I use Pecorino Romano cheese instead of Parmesan because it offers a brighter and more robust flavor that complements the soft creaminess of the ricotta. Pecorino is made from sheep's milk and is not aged as long as Parmesan. Whatever cheese you prefer, you'll be rewarded with a warm, bubbling baking dish full of comfort food goodness.

1 8-ounce package manicotti pasta

15 ounces whole milk ricotta cheese

1 large egg

½ cup shredded Pecorino Romano cheese (or Parmesan)

1 cup shredded mozzarella,

1 tablespoon chopped basil

1 teaspoon salt, divided

1 teaspoon pepper, divided

1 tablespoon olive oil

12 ounces ground beef substitute

2 garlic cloves, minced

½ teaspoon dried oregano

½ teaspoon dried rosemary

1½ cups sliced baby bello or white mushrooms

1 15-ounce can tomato sauce

1. Preheat oven to 350 degrees F.

2. Cook manicotti according to package directions to al dente. You want the pasta tubes to hold together as you pipe in the cheese. Rinse in cold water. Set aside.

3. In a 3-quart mixing bowl, add the ricotta, egg, Pecorino Romano, ½ cup of the mozzarella, the basil, ½ teaspoon salt, and ½ teaspoon pepper. Mix well.

4. In a 10″ skillet, heat the olive oil on medium heat. Add the ground beef substitute, garlic, oregano, rosemary, the remaining ½ teaspoon salt, and ½ teaspoon pepper. Cook until browned.

5. Add the mushrooms. Cook for about 5 minutes.

6. Add the tomato sauce. Simmer on low heat for 10 minutes. Season with salt and pepper.

7. Spoon the ricotta mixture into a plastic sandwich bag. Seal the bag and clip a tiny hole at one corner. Use this bag to pipe the cheese mixture into the center of the manicotti tubes.

8. Spoon a thin layer of the ground beef substitute and mushroom mixture into the bottom of a 9″ x 13″ baking dish. Place the manicotti on the sauce to prevent sticking.

9. Top the filled manicotti with the ground beef substitute and mushroom mixture.

10. Sprinkle the remaining mozzarella on the top. Bake for 30–35 minutes, or until golden brown and bubbly.

Note: If you like a sweeter tomato sauce, add ½–1 tablespoon of sugar to the sauce before adding it to the ground beef substitute mixture.

Cowgirl Chili

SERVES 4

My youngest gal loves a good cup of chili, and this *Cowgirl Chili* recipe is her all-time favorite. It's an easy meal to make in a pinch with either ground beef substitute or ground turkey, and it only takes about thirty minutes from start to finish. When I serve this chili dish, I wrangle up sweet corn bread to serve alongside and shred cheese on the chili to make it even more delicious.

2 tablespoons olive oil

12 ounces ground beef substitute

2–3 garlic cloves, minced

½ teaspoon salt

½ teaspoon coarse ground pepper

1 15-ounce can tomato sauce

1 15-ounce can red kidney beans, drained

½ cup beer (or vegetable stock)

1 tablespoon chili seasoning or chili powder*

1 teaspoon cumin

1 teaspoon paprika

½ teaspoon onion powder

¼ teaspoon ground cayenne (½ teaspoon for hot chili)

Shredded cheddar cheese, for topping

Red onion (diced), for topping

1. In a 10″ skillet heat oil on medium heat. Add the ground beef substitute, garlic, salt, and pepper. Cook until browned.

2. Add the tomato sauce, beans, beer, chili seasoning, cumin, paprika, onion powder, and cayenne. Stir to combine. Cover and simmer on low heat for 20 minutes.

3. Season with salt, and simmer uncovered for 5 minutes.

4. Serve with corn bread and top with cheese or red onion.

Note:* Chili seasoning will include some additional spices like garlic and cayenne pepper, but you can use chili powder instead if that's what you have on hand.

Rolled Tacos

SERVES 4

Rolled Tacos were a childhood treat for me, and still are when I'm home. They are often referred to as taquitos or flautas, but they all mean essentially the same thing. It's hard not to love these delicious meat-filled corn tortillas fried to a perfectly crunchy texture and topped with fresh guacamole, cheddar, and pico de gallo or salsa. Thanks to how easy they are to make at home, and how versatile they are for beef lovers and vegetarians, *Rolled Tacos* make a fun starter, snack, or meal. If you're serving them as a meal, add a green salad or some fresh fruit.

1 tablespoon olive oil, plus additional for pan frying

12 ounces ground beef substitute

½ teaspoon Mexican chili powder

1 garlic clove, minced

¼ teaspoon salt

12 large corn tortillas

2 cups finely shredded cheddar cheese, divided

Guacamole or 1 diced avocado for topping (optional)

Pico de gallo (or salsa)

2 limes

1. In an 8″ skillet, heat 1 tablespoon of the olive oil on medium heat. Add the ground beef substitute, chili powder, garlic, and salt. Cook until browned. Set aside.

2. Warm the corn tortillas in the oven or microwave to make them pliable when rolling.

3. Divide the ground beef substitute mixture among the warm tortillas and top with 1½ cups of cheese. One at a time, roll the tortillas and insert a toothpick to hold them together. Continue the process until all of the tacos have been filled and rolled.

4. In a 10″ skillet, heat a ¼″–½″ layer of vegetable or olive oil on medium heat.

5. Place each taco into the hot oil. Cook all sides until golden brown and crispy, 1–2 minutes each. Place on a paper towel–lined plate.

6. When all the tacos have been cooked, stack them on a platter. Top with guacamole or avocado, remaining cheddar, and pico de gallo or salsa.

7. Cut limes into quarters and use the juice as a garnish.

Lasagna Bolognese

SERVES 4–6

I've learned how to make lasagna on the fly. Here's how I do it: When I make Bolognese, I make enough to keep an extra container in the refrigerator or freezer for future meal prep. So whenever lasagna sounds like a good idea, the sauce is already made, which means I can have lasagna on the table in less than 45 minutes. Enjoy this plant-based beef version with oodles of cheese and all the Italian goodness you'd expect.

12 lasagna pasta sheets

1 15-ounce container ricotta cheese

½ teaspoon Italian seasoning

½ teaspoon dried basil

⅓ cup Pecorino Romano cheese

2 cups shredded mozzarella cheese, divided

1 large egg

¼ teaspoon salt

⅛ teaspoon pepper

2 cups *Bolognese* (see page 113), room temperature

1. Cook the lasagna sheets according to package directions. Rinse in cool water. Set aside.

2. In a 3-quart mixing bowl, combine the ricotta, Italian seasoning, basil, Pecorino, ⅓ cup of the mozzarella, egg, salt, and pepper.

3. Place some of the *Bolognese* onto the bottom of a 7" x 9" baking dish. Add a layer of lasagna sheets.

4. Add a layer of the ricotta mixture and a layer of *Bolognese* on the ricotta. Sprinkle with mozzarella.

5. Continue layering the lasagna sheets, ricotta mixture, *Bolognese*, and mozzarella.

6. Cover with foil. Bake for 15 minutes.

7. Remove the foil. Bake for 20–25 minutes.

8. If you want to brown the top, turn on the broiler for the final minute of baking.

Swedish Meatballs

SERVES 4–6 (15 MEATBALLS)

If you've ever enjoyed swedish meatballs in its creamy traditional form, you'll enjoy this somewhat lighter variation. You'll also notice that the vegetarian meatballs are softer in texture and that the grated onion makes them deliciously moist. This delicious *Swedish Meatballs* recipe includes just the right amount of allspice and nutmeg, adding to its multilayered appeal. Enjoy this dinner even more when you pair it with noodles or rice and crusty bread to sop up the leftover gravy. Need to make this recipe weekday friendly? Make the meatballs ahead of time and warm them up just before putting them in the gravy.

SWEDISH MEATBALLS

¼ cup breadcrumbs

1 tablespoon milk

12 ounces ground beef substitute

1 white onion, grated

¼ teaspoon salt

¼ teaspoon allspice

¼ teaspoon nutmeg

1 large egg

Vegetable oil for frying

Chopped parsley for garnish

GRAVY

1 cup vegetable stock

¼ teaspoon allspice

½ teaspoon salt

¼ teaspoon pepper

½ teaspoon onion powder

½ teaspoon garlic powder

¾ cup sour cream, room temperature

1 tablespoon cornstarch

TO MAKE THE MEATBALLS

1. In a 1.5-quart mixing bowl, combine the bread crumbs and milk.

2. In a 3-quart mixing bowl, combine the ground beef substitute, onion, salt, allspice, nutmeg, and egg. Add the bread crumb mixture. Combine.

3. Using your hands, form small meatballs. Place them on a plate.

4. In a 10″ skillet, heat enough oil to cover the bottom in a thin layer on medium low heat. Add the meatballs. Turn to brown all sides. Place them on a plate. Cover.

5. Place the meatballs in the finished *Gravy* (recipe below). Garnish with the parsley.

TO MAKE THE GRAVY

1. Discard excess oil from cooking the meatballs and use the same 10″ skillet to heat the vegetable stock on medium low heat.

2. Add the allspice, salt, pepper, onion powder, and garlic powder.

3. Whisk in the sour cream. Simmer the gravy on low heat for about 5 minutes.

4. In a 1.5-quart bowl, add cornstarch and 2–3 tablespoons of water. Stir into the gravy to thicken. (Omit this step if the gravy is already thick.)

5. Season with salt and pepper before adding the meatballs.

Note: Because the gravy is made with vegetable stock, not beef stock, it's important to season the gravy as you go.

French Bread Pizza

SERVES 4–6

I'll be honest: I created this *French Bread Pizza* one evening out of desperation for something doughy and savory and fast. I was starving, and so was my family. After taking all of the ingredients I had out of my refrigerator, this happy little miracle happened. This crusty pizza is so good that I make it on the regular. Get creative and garnish these *French Bread Pizzas* with your favorite fresh toppings: How about black olives, jalapeños, artichoke hearts, chopped tomatoes, or Parmesan to name a few?

1 large French bread loaf

3 tablespoons olive oil, divided

1 garlic clove, smashed

½ cup ricotta cheese

¼ teaspoon Italian seasoning

12 ounces ground beef substitute

2 cups pizza sauce

2 cups shredded mozzarella

1. Preheat oven to 425 degrees F.

2. Cut the French bread in half lengthwise and slice into 4–6 pieces.

3. Brush each piece of bread with a teaspoon of olive oil and rub the garlic along the flat sides of the bread.

4. Place on a parchment-lined baking sheet. Toast in the oven for 2–3 minutes, or until golden brown.

5. In a 1.5-quart mixing bowl, combine the ricotta and the Italian seasoning. Season with salt. Set aside.

6. In an 8″–10″ skillet, warm the remaining olive oil on medium heat. Add the ground beef substitute. Cook until browned.

7. Stir in the pizza sauce. Remove from the heat.

8. Spread a layer of ricotta mixture on each bread slice. Spoon on the ground beef substitute mixture. Sprinkle the mozzarella on top.

9. Place the bread back on the baking sheet. Bake for about 10 minutes or until the cheese is melted and bubbly.

Beef and Spinach Pastry Puffs

SERVES 4

Puff pastry is always a good idea. It certainly adds to the melt-in-your-mouth quality of these *Beef and Spinach Pastry Puffs*. I make these satisfying plant-based meat pockets as grab-and-go meals or as a self-serve meal for my busy family. The bonus feature is that they're just as delicious warmed up the next day. Serve with ranch dressing for dipping!

1 tablespoon olive oil

1 onion, diced

6–8 ounces ground beef substitute

2½ cups spinach

½ cup Boursin cheese, any flavor

2 sheets puff pastry, thawed at room temperature

1 large egg

1 tablespoon water

Ranch dressing (optional) for dipping

1. Preheat oven to 350 degrees F.

2. In an 8″ skillet, warm the olive oil on medium heat. Add the onion. Cook until translucent.

3. Add the ground beef substitute. Cook until browned.

4. Add the spinach. Cook until wilted.

5. Remove from the heat, and stir in the Boursin until combined. Season with salt.

6. Cut each pastry sheet in half from corner to corner, creating a triangle.

7. Place the mixture in the middle of the pastry. Fold the pastry over the mixture by bringing one corner to the other. Seal the dough with your fingers.

8. Mix the egg and water together. Brush the egg wash on each pastry.

9. Place on a parchment-lined baking sheet. Bake for 25–30 minutes.

10. Cool for 5 minutes and serve.

Note: Serve these with ranch dressing for dipping.

Stuffed Eggplant

SERVES 4–6

Eggplant Parmesan is a popular meal in my home, but when time is short and I need something that's easy to prep, I make *Stuffed Eggplant*. With the rich flavor of ground beef substitute, a warm layer of pasta sauce, and a blanket of bubbling melted cheese, these little wonders make a quick and tasty meal that your family and friends will enjoy. Pair this recipe with a glass of your favorite Chianti and a side salad, and call it a day!

2 medium-size eggplants

2 tablespoons olive oil

16 ounces ground beef substitute

3 garlic cloves, minced

1 teaspoon salt

½ teaspoon pepper

1 teaspoon chopped oregano
(or ½ teaspoon dried oregano)

½ cup Pecorino Romano cheese,
plus more for garnish

½ cup mozzarella, plus extra for topping

2 cups jarred marinara sauce or
Sunday Sauce (see page 76), divided

¼ cup seasoned bread crumbs

1. Preheat oven to 350 degrees F.

2. Halve the eggplants lengthwise. Scoop out the centers of each half. Leave the sides thick enough to hold their shape while cooking.

3. Cut the eggplant centers into bite-size pieces.

4. In an 8″ skillet, heat the olive oil on medium heat.

5. Add the eggplant pieces. Cook until tender, 1–2 minutes.

6. Add the ground beef substitute, garlic, salt, pepper, and oregano to the eggplant mixture. Cook until browned.

7. Remove from the heat. Place the beef substitute and eggplant mixture in a 3-quart mixing bowl.

8. Stir in the cheeses, 1½ cups of marinara sauce, and the bread crumbs. Season with salt.

9. Spoon the mixture into the eggplant halves. Top with the remaining marinara, and a sprinkle of mozzarella.

10. Place in a 9″ x 13″ greased baking dish.

11. Bake for 40–45 minutes.

12. Garnish with Pecorino Romano cheese.

Note: If your eggplant is too large for one serving, let it cool and slice it in half to create smaller helpings.

Tamale Bake

SERVES 4

Tamales are a family favorite, but making them is no simple task. This *Tamale Bake* is a simple solution. I was introduced to the idea of a casserole-style tamale when I visited my sister and she served it for dinner. I decided to make my own vegetarian version full of plant-based goodness and topped with a delicious sweet corn muffin batter. It's a one-dish dinner that makes it easy to get everyone to the table. You can even add extras like sour cream, cheddar cheese, tomatoes, jalapeños, and green onions.

CORN MUFFIN TOPPING

1½ cups masa harina*
(golden corn flour)

6 tablespoons unsalted butter,
melted

2 tablespoons honey

1 teaspoon salt

1 tablespoon baking powder

1½ cups water, divided

1 cup shredded cheddar cheese

½ cup corn (off the cob or
frozen corn thawed)

TAMALE BAKE

1 tablespoon olive oil

1 sweet onion, diced

12 ounces ground beef substitute

½ teaspoon salt

1 teaspoon minced garlic

1 tablespoon chili powder

1 teaspoon cumin

1 teaspoon paprika

1½ cups tomato puree

1 cup corn (off the cob or
frozen corn thawed)

1 15.5-ounce can black beans,
drained and rinsed

½ cup chopped cilantro

TO MAKE THE MUFFIN TOPPING

1. Preheat oven to 350 degrees F.

2. In a 5-quart mixing bowl stir together the masa, melted butter, honey, salt, baking powder, and 1 cup of the water. Add the next ½ cup of water a little at a time until the batter is smooth.

3. Fold in the cheddar and corn. Set aside.

TO MAKE THE TAMALE BAKE

1. In an 8″ skillet, heat the olive oil on medium heat.

2. Add onion and cook until translucent, about 1 minute.

3. Add the ground beef substitute, salt, garlic, chili powder, cumin, and paprika. Cook until browned, 2–3 minutes.

4. Add the tomato puree, corn, beans, and cilantro. Season with salt and pepper. Cook on medium low heat for 3–4 minutes, until the mixture is simmering.

5. Pour the ground beef substitute mixture into an 8″ x 8″ or 9″ x 9″ baking dish. Top with the corn bread batter, spreading it evenly over the mixture.

6. Bake for 25–30 minutes, or until the top is golden brown and the sides are bubbly.

7. Cool for 5 minutes before serving.

Note:* If you can't find masa harina, you can substitute with finely ground cornmeal. You may need to add additional water to make it more like a muffin batter. Add ¼ cup of water at a time to reach the desired consistency.

Beef and Potato Casserole

SERVES 4–6

I created this recipe out of a sincere love of potatoes au gratin. This *Beef and Potato Casserole* is full of cheesy potatoes and flavorful plant-based beef, making it a satisfyingly delicious breakfast, brunch, or dinner. And, if you're looking for even more protein, top it with a poached egg—it's delicious!

2 tablespoons butter, softened

2 tablespoons olive oil

12 ounces ground beef substitute

½ teaspoon fennel seeds

½ teaspoon salt

½ teaspoon pepper

2 garlic cloves, minced

2–3 large Idaho potatoes, peeled and thinly sliced

2¼ cups shredded Gruyere or sharp cheddar cheese, divided

1½ cups *Cheese Sauce* (see page 54)

1. Preheat oven to 350 degrees F.

2. Spread the butter evenly on the bottom of a 9″ x 13″ baking dish.

3. In a 10″ skillet, heat the olive oil on medium heat.

4. Add the ground beef substitute, fennel, salt, pepper, and garlic. Cook until browned.

5. Layer the casserole by placing ½ of the potatoes in a shingle pattern across the bottom of the baking dish.

6. Sprinkle 1 cup of the shredded cheese on the potatoes and ½ of the ground beef substitute on the cheese.

7. Pour about ¾ cup of *Cheese Sauce* over the meat.

8. Layer again with the remaining potatoes, 1 cup of shredded cheese, ground beef substitute, and the remaining *Cheese Sauce.*

9. Sprinkle the remaining ¼ cup of shredded cheese on the top.

10. Bake for 30–35 minutes, or until the top is golden brown and bubbly. Season with salt and pepper.

Note: To keep your potatoes from turning color while making this recipe, place them in salted milk. If reheating the *Cheese Sauce,* add a few tablespoons of heavy cream or half-and-half while warming to keep it creamy and easier to spread over the potatoes.

INDEX